Opening the CAGE

Opening the CAGE invites you to embark on a transformative journey within the world of education, unveiling a powerful framework to nurture the wellbeing of staff that will not only retain valuable educators but create positive learning environments, ensure academic success and address student needs.

The CAGE framework – representing Communication, Appreciation, Growth and Development, and Empathy and Support – offers a fresh, holistic perspective on addressing the often-overlooked needs of teachers, encapsulating the key components of wellbeing. Through compelling real-world examples, research-based insights and practical strategies, the book explores the profound impact of teacher wellbeing on the quality of education, before drawing inspiration from best practices in different sectors – from sport to business – to provide a roadmap for creating a more positive and productive educational environment.

Whether you are a member of staff in a school seeking to reignite your passion for teaching, a school leader aiming to enhance staff morale or a policymaker dedicated to improving educational outcomes, this book empowers you with the tools to prioritise and foster teacher wellbeing.

Adam Gillett is Associate Vice Principal of Penistone Grammar School and Development Specialist at Minds Ahead. Adam teaches on the School Leadership in Mental Health MA at Leeds Beckett University and speaks regularly at conferences around the country. In 2024, Adam won the Inspirational Teacher Award for his work in the field of mental health in education.

'*Opening the CAGE* is a breath of fresh air for school leaders navigating the pressures of staff wellbeing. Adam Gillett blends powerful insights from education, business and sport into a practical, flexible framework that works. The CAGE approach is honest, thoughtful and packed with real-life examples that make you reflect and rethink. It's a must-read for anyone serious about building a school culture where staff feel valued, supported and able to thrive.'

Dean Johnstone, *CEO of Minds Ahead*

'Reflecting upon his extensive teaching and leadership experience with admirable honesty, Adam Gillett takes a creative approach to envisaging schools as happy places to work by drawing upon stories from a range of professions and industries. This book will make you think differently about what you do and remember why you went into teaching in the first place. *Opening the CAGE* is a must-read for school leaders and teachers who understand that teacher wellbeing lies at the heart of thriving schools.'

Tom Dobson, *Professor of Education, York St John University*

Opening the CAGE

A Framework for Teacher Wellbeing

Adam Gillett

Designed cover image: Getty Images

First published 2026
by Routledge
4 Park Square, Milton Park, Abingdon, Oxon OX14 4RN

and by Routledge
605 Third Avenue, New York, NY 10158

Routledge is an imprint of the Taylor & Francis Group, an informa business
© 2026 Adam Gillett

The right of Adam Gillett to be identified as author of this work has been asserted in accordance with sections 77 and 78 of the Copyright, Designs and Patents Act 1988.

All rights reserved. No part of this book may be reprinted or reproduced or utilised in any form or by any electronic, mechanical, or other means, now known or hereafter invented, including photocopying and recording, or in any information storage or retrieval system, without permission in writing from the publishers.

Trademark notice: Product or corporate names may be trademarks or registered trademarks, and are used only for identification and explanation without intent to infringe.

British Library Cataloguing-in-Publication Data
A catalogue record for this book is available from the British Library

ISBN: 9781032781341 (hbk)
ISBN: 9781032781334 (pbk)
ISBN: 9781003486329 (ebk)

DOI: 10.4324/9781003486329

Typeset in Optima
by Deanta Global Publishing Services, Chennai, India

This book is for Bella and George. Always try, be kind and stick together.
And for Katrina, without whose support I couldn't have written it.

Contents

Foreword   viii
Acknowledgements   x
About the Author   xi
A Note from the Author   xii

Chapter 1 Opening the CAGE   1

Chapter 2 Structure   24

Chapter 3 Leading   44

Chapter 4 Strengths-Based Approach   61

Chapter 5 Communication   80

Chapter 6 Appreciation   103

Chapter 7 Growth and Development   136

Chapter 8 Empathy   156

Conclusion   175
Index   190

Foreword

What is the most important factor for schools to consider to ensure their pupils thrive? For me, the answer is straightforward: happy teaching staff.

But with increasing accountability systems, and mounting external pressure on schools to perform, it is easy to lose sight of this. As external pressure becomes internal pressure, teachers become overworked, underappreciated and stressed, and, in many instances, they become unable to work.

So what should schools do to avoid this all-too-common scenario? If you're reading this foreword now, I'd suggest you're already on the right track.

What I particularly like about *Opening the CAGE* is its creative approach. As Adam outlines in his Introduction, all too often the teaching profession can feel siloed from the rest of society, the practices in schools somehow different from other professional and service industries. This siloing is, of course, part of the problem. The teaching profession becomes isolated, only ever talked about when things go wrong. Internal pressure build, and teachers in schools feel isolated too.

But the reality is that teaching as a profession has so many similarities with other professions and industries. As a football fan, I love that early on in this book there's story about how the manager Carlo Ancelotti recognised the individual talent of his striker Zlatan Ibrahimović, and how, in teaching, leaders need to do the same: that is, take a strengths-based approach and appreciate the talents of their teachers and build the school around them.

Such transdisciplinary thinking can help us view our practice and leadership differently. In the world of the arts, this is sometimes referred to as defamiliarisation: enabling us to see what has become habitual and taken for granted in a new and different light. By taking a transdisciplinary approach, *Opening the CAGE* can help you to defamiliarise your practice – help you to see what you might have lost sight of, what we all sometimes forget, with the noise that surrounds education.

What I also like about the book is that it offers practical suggestions for whole school improvement by fostering communication, appreciation, growth and empathy. There are key questions for you to consider, strategies for you to implement and a continual understanding that these strategies will always need to be contextualised, dependent on you and the brilliant teachers with whom you work. Opening the CAGE in your school will really help you and your teachers to be happy, allowing your pupils to thrive.

Tom Dobson
Professor of Education, York St John University

Acknowledgements

I want to thank the publishers and, in particular, Clare Ashworth, for their support, guidance and feedback. I also want to thank Paul Crook for his support in allowing me to explore the world of wellbeing, and all the staff at Penistone Grammar School who inspired this book. Big thanks to Dean Johnstone at Minds Ahead for his guidance and Tom Dobson for his foreword.

I finally want to thank my parents for their constant and never-changing support, my brother and sister, my family and all my friends. Without your support, this would never have occurred.

About the Author

Adam is Associate Vice Principal: Personal Development at a large (1,900 students) secondary school in South Yorkshire, as well as a Business Development Specialist for Minds Ahead, a non-profit mental health organisation. As well as leading on Personal Development across the school, he also leads on mental health, charity and staff wellbeing – his three major passions. He is also a teacher of history to GCSE and politics at A level. Prior to leading Personal Development, Adam was Assistant Principal in charge of Inclusion for eight years, covering safeguarding as Designated Safeguarding Lead as well as behaviour, attendance, mental health and pastoral care.

Adam has a first-class honours degree in History and Politics from Newcastle University where he won the William Laurence Burn Award for outstanding achievement. Adam was then awarded a fully funded master's in history from the Arts and Humanities Research Council which he completed with distinction. After completing his teaching qualification, he worked his way up to Associate Vice Principal and has worked in Barnsley for 14 years.

Adam recently completed the MA in School Leadership in Mental Health and Wellbeing, which he says is one of his proudest achievements. He was also incredibly proud of his school being awarded the Gold Award for Mental Health from Leeds Beckett University. This has included introducing staff and student wellbeing ambassadors, engaging 23 external agencies and developing an in-depth quality assurance system. Adam now speaks around the country on staff and student mental health.

Adam is a proud dad of two children, a bad but committed runner, a fan of a variety of sports including, to his discredit, being a Sheffield Wednesday fan. He has travelled the world with his wife Katrina, including Asia, Africa, Australasia, North America and Europe. He is an avid reader, film devotee and a fan of indie music. He can often be found running in the Peak District by his Sheffield home, listening to the latest indie music and avoiding news of Sheffield Wednesday's latest loss!

A Note from the Author

In writing this book, I have purposely gone beyond the four walls of education and used case studies from various fields such as technology, retail and sports. Too often, teaching books feel insular, circling around the same old examples and theory, and can be, frankly, boring. When we take a step back and look at other sectors facing challenges similar to the ones in schools, we may find useful strategies that are adaptable and even transformational. We need not conduct a fresh study of the concept for staff wellbeing. There are leaders outside of academia who have instilled communication, appreciation, empathy, accountability and trust into their organisations. They have shown us what works and what does not work.

Focusing on staff wellbeing doesn't mean lowering standards or compromising on the high expectations we have for our pupils; in fact, it's quite the opposite. Focusing on the wellbeing of staff creates the foundation for better teaching, deeper engagement and stronger student outcomes. When staff are well supported, resilient and flexible, they are much better placed to deliver their best in the classroom, manage challenges and maintain effective and high standards of teaching and learning. By investing in an environment in which teachers feel valued and empowered, we're investing in students' success. When teachers feel supported, they can inspire students more, model perseverance and create a rigorous and caring classroom atmosphere. Staff wellbeing and student success are not a trade-off but two sides of the same coin, mutually reinforcing each other.

This book contains stories of how leaders have used one or more aspects of the CAGE approach to engage their teams, cultivate resilience and drive their employees to perform at their best. Look at Ed Catmull, a creative who set up a psychologically safe culture at Pixar, where creativity thrived precisely because people felt safe to fail. Another example is Angela Ahrendts who made Burberry a purpose-driven and community-based brand. These leaders not only spoke of empathy as a value but also integrated it into the practices and culture of their organisation. So I think school leaders can learn valuable lessons from other organisations. And they can use these lessons to lift staff morale and help impact the retention and recruitment crisis in schools.

In line with this, I have made countless mistakes both as a leader and as a person when dealing with staff. I have at times acted impulsively, not thought through my decisions, implemented changes that have backfired. I still make errors. But that is what this book is all about – doing your best to try to make a difference.

Additionally, you'll see that I include reflective questions at the end of every chapter. I hope this book will be helpful and useful, and that you can take the time to reflect deeply on your own thoughts and perceptions, your life and your school setting. You can't just pick this up and implement it – it's not prescriptive. It is a collection of principles, which can be updated and flexible. Some methods will fit your environment better than others, and some may encourage you to reflect on your current methods. The idea is not to adopt a specific type of leadership style as much as it is to encourage you to assess your own leadership with fresh eyes. Use what is useful and understand why you do what you do.

The book doesn't suggest quick fixes or a sticking-plaster approach, but rather a practice of leadership that is intentionally relying on empathy, clarity and reflection. If we get more exposure to other people's different way of thinking, we can bring relevant and impactful changes in our own environment. I hope that you will use these different examples to help create a culture that uplifts your staff members, while giving them support to grow and enhance their wellbeing. When you do this, you will help build a school community for a common purpose and a greater commitment to growth.

Chapter 1
Opening the CAGE

Imagine walking into one of Google's innovative campuses, a hub of creativity where the focus on both employee satisfaction and customer experience permeates every corner. Leadership, driven by an unyielding commitment to innovation and wellbeing, operates with a shared purpose: to enhance the experience at every possible touchpoint. This guiding principle, deeply embedded in Google's culture, has propelled the company to the forefront of global technology. Central to this success is the 'flywheel effect' – a concept where initial momentum builds upon itself, creating an unstoppable force that drives continuous improvement and growth.

Now, imagine if we applied this same level of dedication and strategic thinking to the realm of staff wellbeing in schools. What if school leaders adopted an 'obsession' with the wellbeing of their staff akin to Google's commitment to innovation and wellbeing? The potential for transformative impact is immense. By prioritising the health, happiness and professional fulfilment of teachers and support staff, schools can create an environment where the educational flywheel spins with ever-increasing momentum.

In this book, we will explore the critical importance of staff wellbeing in educational settings, drawing parallels to the business and sporting world's most successful strategies. Just as Google's relentless focus on the customer drives its success, a school's unwavering commitment to staff wellbeing can foster a thriving educational community. Through a detailed examination of effective practices, case studies and actionable insights, we will uncover how schools can build their own flywheel of wellbeing – one that continually gains speed and efficacy, resulting in a vibrant, supportive and high-performing educational environment.

By embracing this approach, schools can cultivate a culture where staff feel valued, supported and motivated. This, in turn, enhances their capacity to deliver exceptional education, nurturing students who are not only academically proficient but also emotionally resilient and socially responsible.

DOI: 10.4324/9781003486329-1

As we embark on this journey, let us consider how the principles of customer obsession and the flywheel effect can be harnessed to revolutionise staff wellbeing in schools, setting a new standard for educational excellence.

Taking an approach inspired by Google's principles may seem alien to senior leadership teams (SLTs) in schools across the world due to the traditionally insular nature of the education sector. Unlike the dynamic and often cross-industry exchanges prevalent in the business world, education has long operated within its own unique set of norms, practices and values. This insularity means that educational leaders are not typically accustomed to borrowing strategies from other sectors, especially those as distinct as e-commerce and global commerce.

Furthermore, the core mission of education – focused on teaching, learning and student development – often seems fundamentally different from the profit-driven goals of businesses like Google. In fact, some of their business practices may be frowned upon in lots of other professions, not just education. The notion of applying business strategies to educational settings can thus appear incongruent, if not entirely inappropriate. Staff might worry that such an approach could undermine the intrinsic values of education, prioritising metrics and efficiencies over the holistic development of students.

Moreover, the language and concepts used in business, such as 'customer obsession' and the 'flywheel effect', can feel foreign and perhaps even uncomfortable within the educational environment. The idea of viewing staff wellbeing through a lens akin to customer satisfaction might be seen as reducing complex human needs and relationships to basic, straightforward terms. This resistance is compounded by a lack of exposure to the potential benefits that cross-sector innovation can bring. Schools often visit each other to explore best practice. How often do schools visit organisations in other sectors?

As this book will demonstrate, there is much to gain from adopting and adapting successful strategies from other fields. By understanding and addressing the initial discomfort and scepticism, SLTs can open the door to transformative practices that prioritise staff wellbeing, ultimately fostering an environment where both staff and students thrive. Embracing a more open, cross-sector approach can lead to innovative solutions that enhance the educational experience in profound and lasting ways.

This book aims to draw from the world of business, sport and other sectors to introduce innovative strategies and practices that can significantly enhance staff wellbeing in schools. By exploring successful approaches from these diverse fields, we can identify and adapt techniques that foster a supportive and thriving work environment for staff. The goal is to break free from the traditionally insular nature of education and embrace a broader perspective that values cross-sector collaboration. Through this lens, we can discover new ways to prioritise and improve the health, happiness and professional fulfilment of school staff, ultimately creating a more effective and resilient educational system.

To illustrate the power of the above, let's look at three examples from the world of sport. Learning from individuals in sport can provide valuable insights into staff wellbeing in education. Athletes and coaches often face intense pressure, requiring them to develop strategies for maintaining their physical and mental health. These strategies can be adapted to support the wellbeing of teachers and school staff, who also operate in high-stress environments. By examining the leadership styles and personal resilience of successful sports figures, we can uncover principles that promote a positive and supportive work culture in schools.

As an example of how we can learn from sectors outside education, let's start by looking at some examples from the world of sport. From a case study of Phil Jackson, the inspiration behind the Chicago Bulls' success in the 1990s, to the leadership of Carlo Ancelotti and Serena Williams, we can draw valuable lessons for fostering staff wellbeing in educational settings.

Insights from Phil Jackson

In the annals of basketball coaching, Phil Jackson stands as a leader who orchestrated success through a deep understanding of his players. One of the most intriguing chapters in Jackson's coaching journey unfolded with the enigmatic Dennis Rodman during their time together with the Chicago Bulls. This unique partnership, which included allowing Rodman occasional trips to Las Vegas to blow off steam, offers profound lessons for fostering staff wellbeing in schools. By examining the dynamics between Jackson and Rodman, we can extract principles that transcend the basketball court, providing valuable insights into leadership and individualised support.

Phil Jackson's coaching philosophy thrived on embracing the unconventional, and Dennis Rodman epitomised this approach. Recognising Rodman's unorthodox yet effective playing style, Jackson celebrated his uniqueness rather than attempting to conform. In schools, leaders can draw a parallel by appreciating the diverse teaching styles, methodologies and personalities within their staff. Acknowledging and understanding the unconventional can lead to a more inclusive and harmonious working environment.

A notable episode in the Jackson–Rodman saga was the permission granted for Rodman to take brief excursions to Las Vegas during the season. This decision, rooted in trust, illustrates Jackson's belief in providing autonomy to his players. Translating this to the school context, empowering staff with a sense of autonomy fosters a culture of trust. Allowing flexibility and recognising the professional judgement of teachers contributes to a more motivated and satisfied staff.

Phil Jackson's leadership extended beyond the basketball court; he recognised the importance of catering to the personal needs of his players. In Rodman's case, occasional trips to Las Vegas served as a release valve, allowing him to recharge mentally and emotionally. In schools, acknowledging and accommodating the personal needs of staff is crucial for staff wellbeing. Providing avenues for downtime, professional development opportunities aligned with personal interests, and a supportive work–life balance can contribute to overall satisfaction and effectiveness.

While allowing Rodman's Vegas breaks, Jackson maintained clear communication and established boundaries. This open dialogue ensured that personal choices did not compromise team dynamics. In schools, effective communication between leadership and staff, along with clearly defined boundaries, is essential. Establishing channels for open dialogue prevents misunderstandings, aligns expectations and contributes to a positive and collaborative working environment.

The collaboration between Phil Jackson and Dennis Rodman provides a compelling narrative of leadership, trust and recognising individual needs. By embracing the unconventional, fostering trust, recognising personal needs and maintaining open communication, Jackson's coaching philosophy offers valuable insights into creating a harmonious and supportive environment. For schools, these principles can guide leaders in nurturing staff wellbeing, promoting a positive school culture and ultimately enhancing the overall success of the educational institution.

Insights from Serena Williams

Serena Williams, one of the greatest tennis players of all time, offers a compelling example of leadership and resilience that can be applied to staff wellbeing in education. Throughout her career, Serena has demonstrated an unwavering commitment to excellence, both on and off the court. Her journey provides valuable lessons for fostering a supportive and empowering environment in schools.

Serena's leadership is evident in her advocacy for gender equality and social justice. She has been a vocal proponent of equal pay for female athletes and has used her platform to challenge societal norms and biases. This commitment to fairness and support for her peers highlights the importance of creating an inclusive and equitable environment. In schools, leaders can draw a parallel by ensuring that all staff members feel valued and supported, regardless of their background or teaching style.

One of the most notable aspects of Serena's career is her ability to balance personal and professional demands. She has openly discussed the challenges of being a working mother and the importance of setting boundaries to maintain her wellbeing. This approach underscores the significance of acknowledging and accommodating the personal needs of staff. By providing flexibility and understanding, school leaders can help teachers and support staff achieve a healthy work–life balance, leading to greater job satisfaction and effectiveness.

Serena's resilience in the face of adversity is another key lesson for school leaders. She has faced numerous challenges, including injuries, biased officiating and public scrutiny, yet she has consistently demonstrated mental toughness and grace. This resilience can inspire school leaders to support their staff through difficult times, fostering a culture of perseverance and mutual support.

Effective communication has also been a hallmark of Serena's career. She has maintained open dialogue with her coaches, teammates and the media, ensuring that her voice is heard and her needs are met. In schools, clear and open communication between leadership and staff is essential for building trust and preventing misunderstandings. Establishing channels for regular feedback and dialogue can contribute to a positive and collaborative working environment.

Serena Williams' leadership and advocacy provide a powerful narrative of resilience, fairness and effective communication. By embracing these principles, school leaders can nurture staff wellbeing, promote a positive school culture and ultimately enhance the overall success of the educational institution.

Insights from Carlo Ancelotti and Zlatan Ibrahimović

Serena Williams' story is not unique; it is mirrored in how Carlo Ancelotti handled the enigmatic Zlatan Ibrahimović. In the realm of football management, the art of extracting the best from each player is a skill mastered by a select few. One such individual is Carlo Ancelotti, renowned for his ability to nurture talent and orchestrate success on the pitch. He is one of the most successful managers of all time, winning the Champions League five times as a manager and twice as a player, as well as numerous league titles in the UK, Spain, Germany and Italy. An exemplary illustration of Ancelotti's managerial prowess is his tenure at Paris Saint-Germain (PSG), where he masterfully unlocked the potential of the enigmatic Zlatan Ibrahimović. Just as Ancelotti elevated Ibrahimović's game to new heights, the principles behind this can be translated into the broader context of unlocking the potential of individuals in education.

Carlo Ancelotti's success with Zlatan Ibrahimović began with a fundamental understanding of the player. Ancelotti recognised that Ibrahimović was not merely a cog in the football machinery but a unique blend of skill, personality and untapped potential. This realisation is crucial when considering staff wellbeing in schools – recognising that each member of staff is a distinct individual with their own strengths, challenges and aspirations.

One of Ancelotti's key strengths lies in his ability to foster an environment of trust. He established a relationship with Ibrahimović based on mutual respect and open communication, encouraging the player to express himself freely on and off the pitch. Translating this into the school setting, creating a culture of trust is essential for staff wellbeing. Staff must feel supported and empowered to voice their ideas, concerns and ambitions, fostering a collaborative atmosphere where everyone's contributions are valued.

Ancelotti strategically utilised Ibrahimović's strengths to benefit the team. Recognising the striker's unique skill set, Ancelotti tailored his tactical approach to capitalise on Ibrahimović's abilities, resulting in an outstanding collaborative performance. In schools, acknowledging and leveraging the strengths of staff can lead to a harmonious and effective working environment. How often do we adopt a system which we ask staff to adapt to, rather than building a system around the skills of our staff? By providing opportunities for professional growth in areas where individuals excel, schools can ensure that each staff member contributes optimally to the collective success.

Ancelotti's approach with Ibrahimović extended beyond tactical considerations. He invested time and effort in understanding the player's personal and professional aspirations, providing individualised support to facilitate growth. Similarly, supporting staff wellbeing in schools involves recognising and addressing the unique needs of staff. Professional development programmes, mentorship and wellbeing initiatives tailored to individual requirements can contribute to a more fulfilled and engaged teaching staff.

Applying Lessons to Education

In the stories of Carlo Ancelotti and Zlatan Ibrahimović, Serena Williams, or Phil Jackson and Dennis Rodman, we find a rich source of inspiration for unlocking the potential within individuals. By understanding, trusting, leveraging strengths and providing personalised support, these approaches have transcended their respective sports to offer valuable insights into maximising human potential. In the world of education, these principles can guide school leaders in creating environments where staff thrive, ensuring a positive impact on student outcomes and the overall success of the institution.

At the heart of these narratives lies the profound impact of recognising and embracing individuality. Carlo Ancelotti's success with Ibrahimović stemmed from understanding the player's unique qualities, fostering an environment that allowed him to flourish. Similarly, Phil Jackson's ability to harness Dennis Rodman's unconventional talents, even permitting occasional trips to Las Vegas, underscored the power of accepting and leveraging individual strengths. Serena Williams' career exemplifies this as well, with her advocacy for gender equality and her ability to balance personal and professional demands, highlighting the importance of recognising and supporting individual needs.

The parallels extend to the importance of trust and autonomy in leadership. Ancelotti trusted Ibrahimović's abilities, providing the freedom to express himself on the field. In a parallel vein, Jackson's trust in Rodman's professionalism, even during his Vegas escapades, emphasised the significance of empowering individuals with autonomy. Serena Williams' resilience and open communication with her coaches and teammates further illustrate the value of trust and autonomy. This trust, coupled with clear communication and boundaries, formed the cornerstone of successful collaborations.

Furthermore, all these stories emphasise the necessity of recognising and accommodating personal needs. Ancelotti's understanding of Ibrahimović's psyche, Jackson's acknowledgement of Rodman's need for occasional breaks, and Williams' advocacy for work–life balance spotlight the importance of considering individual wellbeing within a team dynamic.

As schools grapple with the multifaceted challenge of staff wellbeing, the Ibrahimović–Ancelotti, Rodman–Jackson and Williams narratives offer invaluable lessons. Leaders in education can glean insights into fostering a positive environment by appreciating the diversity among their staff, building trust, allowing autonomy and recognising and accommodating personal needs. The convergence of these stories underscores the universal principles that guide effective leadership, transcending the boundaries of sports and professions. In the realm of education, acknowledging and celebrating the individual strengths and needs of staff can pave the way for a harmonious, supportive and successful school community.

So Why Is This Important Now?

As educational leaders and staff, we bear the significant responsibility of shaping the future through the development of the current and upcoming generations. This responsibility transcends geographical boundaries, and the weight of these expectations places a considerable burden on leaders in education worldwide. While most teachers are not drawn to the profession solely for financial rewards, and while the allure of holidays is undeniable, these factors do not adequately compensate for the demanding nature of daily life in schools. Consequently, the wellbeing of teachers should be among the highest priorities in the field of education.

Unfortunately, recent years have witnessed a concerning decline in teacher wellbeing, evident in heightened rates of occupational stress and burnout (Aloe et al., 2014) and decreased life satisfaction (Ofsted, 2019). Disturbingly, there has been a 4 per cent increase in long-term mental health issues among teachers (Allen et al., 2021; Jerrim & Sims, 2021). Even more alarming is the fact that a significant number of our colleagues choose to leave the profession within their initial five years due to the adverse impact on their mental health and wellbeing (Ofsted, 2019).

These concerning trends, coupled with global concerns about teacher retention (OECD, 2018), emphasise the urgency for policymakers and employers to prioritise teacher wellbeing. Without addressing these issues, we risk the teaching profession becoming a revolving door, constantly training and investing in teachers only to watch them leave. Moreover, it is essential to recognise that stressed teachers do not make effective staff. The wellbeing of the staff directly impacts students' attainment and progress. Additionally, the financial cost of hiring cover for stressed or absent teachers' further strains school budgets, affecting the most crucial stakeholders: our students.

Teacher Wellbeing: A Closer Examination:

Teacher wellbeing encompasses various dimensions, from material aspects to relational and subjective factors (Disabato et al., 2016). However, measuring wellbeing is challenging due to its inherently subjective nature (Dodge et al., 2012). Regrettably, in education policies, wellbeing measurements are often overlooked, with limited attention from central government authorities. The lack of cohesive policies only exacerbates stress on teachers, as evidenced by the post-2020 GCSE results algorithm debacle.

A recent survey conducted in 2021 revealed a stark reality: 44 per cent of teachers in England and Wales felt unsupported by their schools regarding wellbeing. Furthermore, 53 per cent contemplated leaving the profession due to wellbeing concerns and mental distress (Education Support, 2021). Despite increased awareness and the implementation of wellbeing policies, staff continue to grapple with stress, anxiety, excessive workloads and elusive work–life balance (Education Support, 2021). While leadership teams strive to provide support, available guidance often falls short of addressing wellbeing holistically, overlooking best practices from other industries and leaving a gap in understanding and supporting wellbeing. The recent Department of Education taskforce offers some hope, although the number of CEOs outnumbering the number of teachers on the taskforce is of significant concern (School's Week, 2023).

The consequences of diminishing teacher wellbeing extend far beyond the individual, negatively impacting teacher retention, professional quality and the social and academic development of students (Turner & Thielking, 2020). It is crucial to recognise that teachers sometimes feel isolated and trapped, leading to devastating outcomes. In light of our profound understanding of the importance of nurturing positive learning environments, advocating for the prioritisation of teacher wellbeing is now more critical than ever, particularly in the post-COVID-19 era, where the pressures on our profession have intensified.

A pivotal moment in the recognition of the severity of poor teacher mental health came with the Organisation for Economic Co-operation and Development's (OECD) urgent call in 2019 for policymakers and researchers to join forces in addressing the declining job satisfaction among staff, which includes mental health and wellbeing concerns. Indeed, recent studies, such as the Department for Education's 'Working Lives of Teachers and Leaders – Wave 1' (Department for Education, 2023), have revealed alarming statistics, with a staggering 86 per cent of teachers reporting stress in their work life and a significant portion considering leaving the profession due to unsustainable workloads. These findings underscore the urgent need for proactive measures to support teacher mental health.

Similarly, smaller-scale surveys, such as the Teacher Wellbeing Index (TWI) (Education Support, 2022), have highlighted the pervasive impact of work-related stress on teacher mental health, with a substantial proportion attributing their poor mental health to work-related factors. Senior leaders, in particular, bear a disproportionate burden, with higher levels of acute stress reported among this group. The detrimental effects of these stressors are not confined to individual staff but reverberate throughout the school environment, impacting student wellbeing and educational outcomes.

As we navigate the post-pandemic landscape, characterised by unprecedented challenges and uncertainties, the imperative to prioritise teacher mental health has never been clearer. This book endeavours to unpack the multifaceted dimensions of this critical issue, offering insights into effective leadership strategies and interventions that foster a culture of psychological safety, engagement and wellbeing. By equipping staff and school leaders with evidence-based practices and actionable strategies, we aspire to cultivate resilient and thriving school communities where both staff and students can flourish.

Nurturing Teacher Wellbeing: A Holistic Approach:

Enhancing teacher wellbeing involves multiple levels, from national policies to individual teacher actions (Viac & Fraser, 2020). In this intricate landscape, our focus is on school-level wellbeing support for schoolteachers in England. Our approach aligns with theoretical models that emphasise the pivotal role of school environments in nurturing teacher wellbeing (Jennings & Greenberg, 2009; Liu & Onwuegbuzie, 2018; Viac & Fraser, 2020).

As leaders and staff, it is our shared responsibility to address the challenges facing teacher wellbeing collaboratively. By prioritising the wellbeing of our teachers, we not only retain valuable staff but also create positive learning environments, ensure academic success, address student needs and bolster their own wellbeing.

Let us work together to cultivate a profession where teacher wellbeing is a cornerstone, ensuring a brighter future for both staff and students. Let's open the CAGE.

Opening the CAGE: A Framework for Teacher Wellbeing

In our pursuit of comprehensively addressing teacher wellbeing, we need to 'open the CAGE'. This is a conceptual model designed to encapsulate the key components of wellbeing and offer a holistic perspective. CAGE stands for Communication, Appreciation, Growth and Development, and Empathy and Support. Each element of this framework plays a pivotal role in understanding and enhancing the wellbeing of teachers. The CAGE framework, inspired by principles from business, sports and other sectors, emphasises the importance of cross-field learning and how techniques from diverse industries can enhance staff wellbeing in schools. This framework will be explored in depth throughout the book, as each chapter unpacks its elements and how they relate to staff wellbeing in various contexts.

C: Communication

Effective communication among staff members and with school leadership is essential for addressing concerns, sharing resources and building a supportive community. Open and transparent communication channels facilitate the exchange of ideas, collaboration and problem-solving. When teachers feel that their voices are heard and valued, it contributes significantly to their wellbeing.

A: Appreciation

Recognising and appreciating the efforts and contributions of teachers and staff can boost morale and overall wellbeing. A culture of appreciation includes acknowledging achievements, expressing gratitude and providing constructive feedback. When teachers feel appreciated, it positively impacts their job satisfaction and motivation.

G: Growth and Development

Providing opportunities for professional growth and development helps staff members feel valued and can enhance their job satisfaction. Offering access to training, mentorship and opportunities for career advancement demonstrates a commitment to their personal and professional growth. It also contributes to a sense of purpose and fulfilment in their roles.

E: Empathy and Support

Cultivating a culture of empathy and support within the school community allows staff to feel heard, understood and cared for in times of personal or professional challenges. Providing emotional support and empathy demonstrates a commitment to the wellbeing of teachers. In such an environment, teachers are more likely to navigate stressors and setbacks effectively.

The CAGE framework offers a structured approach to comprehending the multifaceted nature of teacher wellbeing. By exploring the interplay of Communication, Appreciation, Growth and Development, and Empathy and Support, we aim to uncover valuable insights and evidence-based strategies to promote and support teacher wellbeing. In the subsequent sections of this book, we will delve deeper into each component of the CAGE framework, providing an in-depth analysis and recommendations to enhance teacher wellbeing.

Opening the CAGE: The Practice

So how do we open the CAGE in practice? Below are some suggestions, but this framework is designed to be adapted to your own individual needs. The following suggestions offer a starting point, and the upcoming chapters will explore these ideas in greater detail, with practical examples from different educational settings.

Communication

- **Regular staff meetings:** Hold regular staff meetings where teachers can openly discuss concerns, share ideas and provide feedback. Ensure that these meetings are inclusive and encourage participation from all staff members.
- **Listen more, talk less:** When teaching classes, we would not spend an hour at the front talking at them. And yet this is the model adopted in many staff meetings. Think about how you can reduce meetings by using briefing bulletins. Provide informal opportunities for feedback, such as coffee mornings.
- **Feedback mechanisms:** Establish anonymous feedback mechanisms, such as suggestion boxes or online surveys, to allow teachers to express their thoughts and concerns without fear of reprisal. Make staff voice frequent, often and planned. Schools should have a three-year plan for staff wellbeing, and that plan should be punctuated regularly by staff voice.
- **Calendar:** The calendar can make or break a staff body. Where do you put your parents' evenings? On a Thursday, so staff only have one day to get through after? When do you put your open evenings? Do you do an inset the day after so that staff give their all to the night before? Share with your middle leaders and ask them to review it. A poor calendar can make a real difference.
- **Transparent decision-making:** Be transparent about important decisions that affect the school and involve staff in the decision-making process whenever possible. Share the rationale behind decisions and their potential impact on teachers.
- **Accessible leadership:** Make sure that school leadership is approachable and accessible to all staff members. Encourage teachers to reach out when they have questions or need support. Adopt an 'open-door' policy, but make it beyond a policy. Make it a reality.
- **IT systems:** Review the IT systems you have in place. So many schools have systems on systems, which causes confusion and stress. Streamline them as best as possible, amalgamating and working with staff to get the best one for them.

- **Data:** If you collect data, think about when and why. Work with staff so it aligns with curriculum maps and make it as easy as possible. Also, report back to staff what you are using it for.
- **Parents' evening/report writing:** The impact of these is difficult to quantify. Consider how these can be done to support staff. Could they be virtual? Could you encourage soft opportunities to get parents into school (book looks, school shows, meet the teacher) rather than hard ones?

Appreciation

- **Recognition programmes:** Implement recognition programmes that celebrate the achievements and contributions of teachers and staff. Recognise milestones, such as years of service or exceptional performance, with certificates, awards or public acknowledgements.
- **Express gratitude:** Personally express gratitude and appreciation to teachers for their hard work and dedication. A simple thank-you note, a word of praise or a personalised message can go a long way.
- **Peer recognition:** Encourage a culture of peer-to-peer recognition where teachers acknowledge and appreciate each other's efforts. Create opportunities for colleagues to celebrate each other's successes. Think about a Secret Angel system or similar.
- **Appreciate, don't delegate:** If you value what a teacher does in class, do you show it by giving them lots of duties outside of class? Do you make them do detention duty, bus duty, etc.? Where you can avoid this, do. Teachers have the biggest impact in the classroom. Where possible, SLT need to pick up behaviour incidents, do duties and deal with difficult parents. Let the teacher have the impact in the classroom.

Growth and Development

- **Professional development plans:** Work with teachers to create individualised professional development plans that align with their career goals and interests. Provide funding or resources for training, workshops and conferences.
- **Teacher development is different to appraisal:** Scrap formal lesson observations and embrace a culture of support where visiting lessons is

about supporting staff, not judging them. Develop a teacher development plan which focuses on peer coaching to improve teaching and learning. Keep the appraisal programme short and with minimal documentation. Very few teachers value appraisal, and even fewer change how they work with children because of it.
- **Mentorship programmes:** Establish mentorship programmes where experienced teachers mentor newer ones. This not only supports professional growth but also fosters a sense of belonging and community.
- **Create community:** We focus on a sense of belonging with children – do the same with staff. If you have a house system, make sure staff feel part of it by doing competitions and fun quizzes for staff.
- **Career pathways:** Create clear pathways for career advancement within the school, such as opportunities for teacher leadership roles, department head positions or curriculum development roles. Encourage teachers to pursue leadership opportunities.
- **Differentiate:** Have a differentiated plan for staff at different stages of their career. For example, an early career teacher (ECT) may need a small fund to buy items for their classroom, whereas a middle leader may need a day working from home a term to help them prepare curriculum maps. Thinking carefully about what each member of staff may need at different stages of their career means the support is targeted and tailored. Most importantly, it is impactful.
- **Strengths-based approach:** Move away from focusing on what you need to improve on as a school. Instead, emphasise what you do well. Talk about it constantly, and then look at how you can use those strengths to improve other areas. Have a group of staff who are negative and don't buy in? Focus on the staff who do, champion them and get them to support those who don't. Nudge theory is a powerful tool.

Empathy and Support

- **Mental health resources:** Offer access to mental health resources and counselling services for teachers who may be experiencing stress or personal challenges. Promote a stigma-free environment around seeking help. Join something like Westfield Health and promote their services and a number staff can use easily.

- **Flexible work arrangements:** Be flexible with work arrangements when possible, allowing teachers to balance personal and professional responsibilities. This may include options for remote work or flexible hours. Allowing staff to work from home occasionally, with clear expectations on what is achieved, can make such a difference to their mental wellbeing.
- **Wellness programmes:** Implement wellness programmes that focus on physical and mental wellbeing. Offer workshops on stress management, mindfulness and self-care techniques. Ask staff what they would like – free gym membership or a free flu jab may cost, but the impact could be significant.
- **Peer support networks:** Encourage the formation of peer support networks among teachers. These networks can provide emotional support, a sense of belonging and a safe space for sharing experiences.

A lot of leaders will look at some of the above as unachievable. But we have to change our way of thinking, be brave and try to change the culture and climate within our schools. Those schools who do will be at the forefront of a revolution.

Before we look at the CAGE approach, we need to first understand a few fundamentals.

Control What You Can Control

In the realm of staff wellbeing, a crucial principle that resonates across leadership contexts is the mantra 'Control what you can control'. As leaders, we are often confronted with challenges beyond our purview, such as an individual's home life, personal circumstances or lifestyle choices. While these factors undoubtedly impact wellbeing, it's essential to recognise that our sphere of influence is bounded by the structures within our control.

The Serenity to Accept

In business and leadership, this concept finds resonance in the well-known Serenity Prayer, attributed to Reinhold Niebuhr. It encapsulates the wisdom of distinguishing between factors we can control and those beyond our reach:

Grant me the serenity to accept the things I cannot change, courage to change the things I can, and wisdom to know the difference.

This wisdom is particularly pertinent when considering staff wellbeing. Leaders cannot alter the personal lives or lifestyle choices of their team members. However, they can influence and shape the structures, policies and culture within the organisational sphere.

Consider the analogy of an apple orchard. A wise orchardist recognises that while they cannot control external factors like weather conditions, they have a direct influence over the soil quality, irrigation systems and pest control measures. By focusing on optimising these controllable variables, they enhance the overall health of the orchard and the quality of the apples it produces.

In the corporate world, exemplary leaders often embody this principle. A CEO may acknowledge that they cannot control the personal challenges their employees face outside of work. However, they can control the organisational culture, policies and support mechanisms that contribute to a positive work environment.

For instance, a leader can implement flexible work hours, mental health initiatives and avenues for professional development. These structures foster a supportive workplace where employees feel valued and can thrive despite external challenges.

In the educational context, this principle underscores the importance of creating a nurturing school environment. Leaders cannot alter the personal circumstances of their staff, but they can establish structures that prioritise work–life balance, provide professional development opportunities and cultivate a culture of collaboration and support.

By concentrating efforts on what can be controlled within the school's ambit, leaders contribute to an environment where staff wellbeing is prioritised. This approach not only fosters a positive atmosphere but also equips individuals to navigate challenges beyond the school gates more effectively.

In essence, 'Control what you can control' encapsulates a pragmatic and empowering approach to leadership in the pursuit of staff wellbeing. Leaders who recognise and optimise their sphere of influence contribute significantly to the holistic development and resilience of their team members.

Wellbeing vs. Well-Doing

In the realm of staff wellbeing, a fundamental shift is needed – from perceiving it as sporadic events, like a yoga session or occasional treats in the staff room, to embedding it in the everyday culture of the workplace. This paradigm shift revolves around understanding the distinction between 'wellbeing' and 'well doing'.

'Well doing' often involves episodic initiatives – special events, workshops or perks aimed at providing a momentary boost to morale. While these activities can be valuable, relying solely on them can create a 'quick fix' approach to wellbeing. It's akin to addressing symptoms without delving into the root causes of any underlying issues.

In contrast, 'wellbeing' embodies a comprehensive and sustained approach woven into the fabric of daily organisational life. It transcends occasional events, manifesting as a fundamental aspect of the workplace culture. True staff wellbeing is not about a singular yoga session or occasional treats but is embedded in how we operate every day.

Consider the example of Google, renowned not just for its innovative products but also for its exceptional workplace culture. Google doesn't view wellbeing as an isolated event; instead, it's ingrained in the company's DNA. From flexible work hours and mindfulness programmes to on-site fitness centres and healthy food options, Google's approach to wellbeing is pervasive.

Leadership at Google recognises that true wellbeing is a result of the daily experiences employees have at work. It's about fostering an environment where individuals feel supported, valued and motivated each day. This extends beyond perks to include inclusive leadership, open communication and opportunities for professional growth.

In the educational context, the 'wellbeing' approach underscores the importance of creating a daily culture that promotes teacher and staff welfare. It involves regular practices that contribute to a positive and supportive environment. This could encompass collaborative planning sessions, consistent recognition of achievements and open communication channels.

While occasional treats and events have their place, they should complement, not replace, the ongoing commitment to staff wellbeing. Leaders must focus on creating an environment where individuals are not just 'doing well' during special occasions but are consistently supported and thriving in their everyday experiences.

Leaders play a pivotal role in shaping this culture. By prioritising wellbeing in policies, communication and decision-making, leaders signal its importance. It's about creating a workplace where individuals are not just productive but also fulfilled, finding meaning and support in their daily endeavours.

In summary, the shift from 'well doing' to 'wellbeing' is a transformational journey that involves weaving supportive practices into the everyday fabric of the workplace. Leaders who understand this distinction and actively cultivate a culture of wellbeing contribute to a resilient, motivated and fulfilled team.

Teaching Is Tough

Teaching is undoubtedly one of the most challenging professions, demanding a unique blend of skills, resilience and unwavering dedication. Much like coaching a sports team, staff face a myriad of challenges that are inherently woven into the fabric of their roles. Understanding and acknowledging these challenges is essential for fostering a culture of empathy and support within the education community.

The Unique Challenges of Teaching

- **Diverse student needs:** In a classroom, staff encounter a diverse array of student needs, ranging from varying learning styles to distinct socio-economic backgrounds. Navigating this diversity requires a nuanced approach that goes beyond one-size-fits-all teaching methodologies.
- **High stakes:** The impact of teaching extends far beyond the classroom. Staff bear the responsibility of shaping the future by nurturing young minds. The weight of this responsibility, coupled with the external pressures of standardised testing and academic benchmarks, adds an additional layer of stress.
- **Limited resources:** Many teachers grapple with limited resources, be it time, funding or classroom supplies. Balancing the desire to provide the best possible education with these constraints can be a constant juggling act.
- **Emotional strain:** Teaching is an emotionally demanding profession. Staff invest not only in the intellectual growth of their students but also in their social and emotional development. Dealing with a spectrum of emotions, from joy to frustration, is an intrinsic part of the job.

To grasp the unique challenges of teaching, consider the analogy of coaching a sports team. A coach faces the task of honing the skills of individual players, fostering teamwork and navigating the unpredictability of each game. Similarly, teachers must address the individual needs of students, promote a collaborative learning environment and adapt to the dynamic nature of education.

Much like a sports team, a classroom comprises diverse talents and personalities. The coach (teacher) must recognise and leverage these differences to create a harmonious and effective unit. However, in teaching, success is measured not solely by scores or exam grades but also by the growth and development of each individual. Teachers are assessed constantly on matters outside of their control, but for which they take responsibility. Take attendance. Schools can have a huge impact on this, but research shows the biggest impact is the parents. But the school takes the judgement.

The challenges teachers encounter are not meant to deter but to illuminate the unique nature of their profession. Teaching is tough, not because these challenges are insurmountable but because they require a special set of skills and an unwavering commitment to the holistic development of every student.

Recognising the parallels with coaching reinforces the idea that challenges are inherent in any meaningful endeavour. While teaching may be tough, it is also profoundly rewarding. The impact staff have on shaping the future is immeasurable, much like a coach witnessing the growth of their team over a season.

In the face of these challenges, staff find strength in their shared mission – to inspire, educate and empower the next generation. Understanding that teaching is tough but uniquely rewarding fosters a culture of support, collaboration and resilience within the education community.

Navigating Uncharted Waters: Schools in the Era of COVID and Economic Strain

As if the challenges of education weren't substantial enough, schools have been thrust into an era marked by the profound impact of COVID-19 and an escalating cost-of-living crisis. The pandemic, with its disruptive influence on the traditional modes of teaching and learning, has compelled staff to adapt swiftly to remote and hybrid models. The strain on teachers and students alike, juggling technological hurdles and the emotional toll of uncertainty, has been unprecedented.

Simultaneously, the escalating cost-of-living crisis has cast a looming shadow over the educational landscape. Teachers and school staff find themselves grappling with the repercussions of rising prices on everyday essentials, making financial stability an elusive goal. The strain on school budgets, already stretched thin, has intensified, necessitating strategic financial planning to ensure the continuity of quality education.

Amidst these dual challenges, the resilience of staff has shone through, as they strive to provide stability and support to their students. The pandemic has underscored the critical role of schools not just as centres for academic growth but as pillars of emotional and social stability for students facing uncertainties beyond the classroom.

In the face of these trials, it becomes imperative for leaders to acknowledge the added burdens borne by their staff. By fostering a culture of empathy, providing resources for mental health support and implementing practical measures to alleviate financial stress, schools can become beacons of stability in turbulent times. The challenges posed by COVID-19 and economic strains are formidable, but through collaborative efforts and a steadfast commitment to the wellbeing of both staff and students, schools can emerge stronger and more resilient, ready to face whatever uncertainties the future may hold.

As we proceed through this book, each chapter will guide you through the specific elements of the CAGE framework, offering tools and strategies to build and sustain staff wellbeing in your own school.

Reflective Questions

1. How does your current school culture align with the CAGE framework?
2. What strategies from the business or sports world could be adapted to enhance staff wellbeing in your school?
3. Which element of CAGE could be most impactful for your staff right now?

References and Further Reading

Allen, R., Jerrim, J., & Sims, S. (2021). 'How did the early stages of the COVID-19 pandemic affect teacher wellbeing?' UCL Working Paper No. 20-15. https://repec-cepeo.ucl.ac.uk/cepeow/cepeowp20-15.pdf

Aloe, A. M., Amo, L. C., & Shanahan, M. E. (2014). 'Classroom management self-efficacy and burnout: A multivariate meta-analysis.' *Educational Psychology Review, 26*(1), 101–126.

Bock, L. (2015). *Work Rules! Insights from Inside Google That Will Transform How You Live and Lead*. Twelve.

Covey, S. R. (1989). *The 7 Habits of Highly Effective People: Powerful Lessons in Personal Change*. Free Press.

Department for Education. (2023). 'Working lives of teachers and leaders – wave 1.' www.gov.uk/government/publications/working-lives-of-teachers-and-leaders-wave-1

Desimone, L. M. (2009). 'Improving Impact Studies of Teachers' Professional Development: Toward Better Conceptualizations and Measures.' *Educational Researcher, 38*(3), 181–199.

Disabato, D. J., Goodman, F. R., Kashdan, T. B., Short, J. L., & Jarden, A. (2016). 'Different types of well-being? A cross-cultural examination of hedonic and eudaimonic well-being.' Psychological Assessment, 28(5), 471–482.

Dodge, R., Daly, A. P., Huyton, J., & Sanders, L. D. (2012). 'The Challenge of Defining Wellbeing.' *International Journal of Wellbeing, 2*(3), 222–235.

Dunne, C. (n.d.). 'Amazon's Flywheel: What You Can Learn from Jeff Bezos.' xSellco. https://xsellco.com/resources/amazon-flywheel

Education Support. (2021). 'Teacher Wellbeing Index 2021.' www.educationsupport.org.uk/media/qzna4gxb/twix-2021.pdf

Education Support. (2022). 'Teacher Wellbeing Index 2022.' www.educationsupport.org.uk/resources/for-organisations/research/teacher-wellbeing-index

Fullan, M. (2014). *The Principal: Three Keys to Maximizing Impact*. Jossey-Bass.

Goler, L., Gale, J., Harrington, B., & Grant, A. (2018). 'Why People Really Quit Their Jobs.' *Harvard Business Review*. https://hbr.org/2018/01/why-people-really-quit-their-jobs

Hattie, J. (2012). *Visible Learning for Teachers: Maximizing Impact on Learning*. Routledge.

Jennings, P. A., & Greenberg, M. T. (2009). 'The Prosocial Classroom: Teacher Social and Emotional Competence in Relation to Student and Classroom Outcomes.' *Review of Educational Research, 79*(1), 491–525.

Jerrim, J., & Sims, S. (2021). 'When is high workload bad for teacher wellbeing? Accounting for the non-linear contribution of specific teaching tasks.' *Teaching and Teacher Education, 105*, 103395. https://doi.org/10.1016/j.tate.2021.103395

Lencioni, P. (2002). *The Five Dysfunctions of a Team: A Leadership Fable*. Jossey-Bass.

Liu, S., & Onwuegbuzie, A. J. (2018). 'Teacher well-being in the classroom: A cross-national study.' *International Journal of Educational Development, 63*, 110–118.

Maslach, C., & Leiter, M. P. (2016). *Burnout at Work: Causes and Cures*. Psychology Press.

Noddings, N. (2013). *Caring: A Relational Approach to Ethics and Moral Education*. University of California Press.

OECD. (2018). Teaching and Learning International Survey (TALIS): Results. Organisation for Economic Co-operation and Development. www.oecd.org/en/about/programmes/talis.html

Ofsted. (2019). "Teacher well-being at work in schools and further education providers." www.gov.uk/government/publications/teacher-well-being-at-work-in-schools-and-further-education-providers

Schools Week. (2023). 'Revealed: The 14 sector leaders on DfE's workload reduction taskforce.' https://schoolsweek.co.uk/revealed-the-14-sector-leaders-on-dfes-workload-reduction-taskforce

Stone, B. (2013). *The Everything Store: Jeff Bezos and the Age of Amazon*. Little, Brown and Company.

Timperley, H. (2008). *Teacher Professional Learning and Development*. International Academy of Education & International Bureau of Education.

Turner, K., & Thielking, M. (2020). 'Teacher wellbeing: Its effects on teaching practice and student learning outcomes.' *Australian Journal of Education*, 64(2), 227–243.

Viac, C., & Fraser, P. (2020). 'Teacher Wellbeing: A Framework for Data Collection and Analysis.' OECD Education Working Papers, No. 213. OECD Publishing. www.oecd.org/content/dam/oecd/en/publications/reports/2020/01/teachers-well-being_bdafdeaf/c36fc9d3-en.pdf

Chapter 2
Structure

Creating a culture where staff wellbeing thrives requires more than just surface-level initiatives. It's about embedding a sense of community, belonging and purpose into the very fabric of the organisation. Carlo Ancelotti's decision to introduce a café at Paris Saint-Germain is a brilliant example of this principle in action. By giving his players and staff a space to connect informally, he recognised that successful teams are built on relationships that transcend formal structures. This simple café became a powerful tool for cultivating trust, improving communication and breaking down hierarchical barriers.

But the world of sport is not the only place where we can observe the importance of structure in nurturing wellbeing. The business world, particularly forward-thinking companies like Google, has also long understood the link between a well-designed environment and staff performance. Google's famous campus isn't just about quirky features like free food, nap pods or ping-pong tables. Those are often the elements people focus on, but they are symbols of a deeper philosophy. Google designed its workspaces to promote interaction, creativity and, most importantly, employee satisfaction. Just like Ancelotti's café at Paris Saint-Germain, these spaces foster informal exchanges that lead to collaboration and innovation.

Take the example of Google's 'micro-kitchens'. Strategically placed throughout their offices, these are more than just places to grab a snack. They serve as gathering points where employees from different departments naturally bump into each other, sparking conversations that might not happen in a formal meeting. It's in these chance encounters that some of Google's most innovative ideas have been born. The structure of the workspace itself becomes an engine of collaboration and creativity. Google's emphasis on these informal spaces stems from a recognition that the culture they want – a culture of innovation – requires a structure that encourages constant, cross-disciplinary communication.

Similarly, in education, we can draw parallels from schools that have successfully embedded staff wellbeing into their structure. Take, for example, a secondary school in the UK that faced significant staff turnover and burnout. Instead of focusing solely on reactive solutions like stress management workshops, the school leadership implemented a new structure around their staff meetings and collaboration spaces. They carved out protected time each week for teachers to engage in professional dialogue that wasn't tied to immediate classroom issues. Instead of focusing on lesson plans or student assessments, these sessions were about broader pedagogical discussions, peer mentoring and wellbeing check-ins. By creating a space where staff could step back from the demands of their day-to-day roles, the school cultivated a culture where reflection, support and professional growth were prioritised.

What all these examples have in common, whether in sport, business or education, is the understanding that structure is the foundation on which culture is built. A positive culture doesn't emerge by accident – it is crafted through thoughtful, intentional design. This requires more than providing benefits or adding a few perks here and there. It's about embedding opportunities for connection, collaboration and support into the very way the organisation operates.

As a school leader, you might not have the resources to build a Google-style campus or redesign your entire school, but the principles remain the same. Think about the spaces in your school – both physical and temporal – that foster connection. Do staff have time to come together and talk in a meaningful way, outside of meetings focused purely on operational issues? Are there areas in the school where informal, relationship-building interactions can happen naturally?

For instance, you might create a quiet, comfortable staff room that invites people to stay and chat over a coffee. Or you could redesign meeting times to include moments of peer support and professional development that focus not just on immediate concerns but on the long-term wellbeing of your staff. These changes don't have to be expensive or grand, but they do need to be purposeful.

Additionally, smaller successful independent businesses also offer valuable lessons in staff wellbeing. For instance, NextJump, an e-commerce company, has embedded health and wellness into its core principles, offering physical activities, mental health support, and healthy snacks to its employees. Another example comes from a well-known primary school in London, which transformed its approach to staff wellbeing by implementing regular 'Wellbeing Walks' for all employees, from teaching assistants to senior leaders. Every Friday afternoon, staff are encouraged to take a walk around the local park in small groups. These walks are a time to decompress, discuss challenges or simply enjoy time with colleagues without the pressures of the school environment. This small structural change led to a noticeable increase in staff morale and cohesion, with staff reporting that they felt more supported, more connected and better able to manage the stresses of the job.

Ultimately, whether you are leading a school, a small local business, a giant multinational or a sports team, the structures you put in place are powerful signals about what you value. If you want to create a culture of wellbeing, start by examining the spaces and systems in your organisation. Are they aligned with the kind of culture you are trying to build? By prioritising staff wellbeing through thoughtful structural design, you set the stage for an environment where everyone can thrive.

How to Create a Structure

In the realm of education, prioritising staff wellbeing is essential for creating a thriving school environment. To achieve this, leaders must establish a clear direction by crafting an intent statement that emphasises the school's commitment to supporting and valuing staff members. This statement serves as a guiding beacon, informing the development of policies that translate intentions into actionable strategies.

A robust wellbeing policy provides the framework for promoting staff wellbeing by addressing workload management, professional development and support mechanisms. This policy is complemented by protocols and quality assurance mechanisms that ensure consistency and effectiveness. Through feedback loops and ongoing evaluation, schools can continuously refine their practices, ensuring that staff wellbeing remains a top priority and contributing to a positive and supportive school culture.

Intent Statement

Crafting an intent statement on staff wellbeing is a foundational step in building a school culture that prioritises the welfare of its staff members. This statement serves as a declaration of the school's core principles and values regarding staff wellbeing, providing a clear direction for decision-making and action. To create an effective intent statement, educational leaders must engage in a collaborative process that involves input from staff members at all levels.

First and foremost, the intent statement should reflect the school's unwavering commitment to fostering a supportive and nurturing environment where staff members feel respected, supported and valued. It should articulate the belief that staff wellbeing is integral to the overall success and effectiveness of the school community. This may involve acknowledging the diverse needs and experiences of staff members and recognising the importance of creating inclusive practices that promote equity and fairness.

In developing the intent statement, it is essential to involve staff members in the process to ensure their voices and perspectives are heard and considered. This can be achieved through various means, such as surveys, focus groups or facilitated discussions. By actively soliciting input from staff, leaders can gain valuable insights into the specific needs, concerns and aspirations of the school community regarding wellbeing.

The intent statement should also outline specific goals and objectives related to staff wellbeing, providing a roadmap for action and accountability. This may include commitments to implementing supportive policies and practices, fostering a culture of open communication and collaboration, and providing resources and opportunities for professional growth and development.

Ultimately, the intent statement serves as a beacon that guides the school community towards a culture of wellbeing that permeates every aspect of school life. It should inspire and motivate staff members to actively engage in efforts to promote their own wellbeing and that of their colleagues, fostering a sense of collective ownership and responsibility for creating a positive and supportive school environment.

Below is an example of an intent statement you can use and modify. It is important it is tailored to your context, to support your staff.

Moral Purpose

[School Name] is passionate about making a difference to the lives of our staff. We believe in teamwork, working with each other, with teachers and colleagues across the school, and with the wider school community. We act with determination. Whatever issues our staff, their families, the school, our team or the community face, we always support, react and pull together. Finally, we are committed to making a difference; we are not passive players in our colleagues' lives but active participants who can and do make a real difference. These are a reflection of the school's curriculum intent statement and core values, in particular [insert values].

Our moral purpose can therefore be summarised below:

- Teamwork.
- Determination.
- Commitment.

What Effective Staff Wellbeing Mean to Us

- The wellbeing of our staff stays at the centre of every conversation and decision we make.
- When staff are here, we can support and empower them – attendance matters.
- Staff perform best when there are clear systems and expectations.
- We use evidence-based practice to ensure everything we do is impactful.
- The mental health of our staff is of the highest priority.

Let's look at case studies from The Ritz-Carlton, Teach First and Basecamp which show how structured, intentional efforts to support employees can lead to a positive and productive organisational culture.

Insights from The Ritz-Carlton

One remarkable example from the hospitality industry that schools can draw inspiration from is The Ritz-Carlton. Known globally for its luxury services, The Ritz-Carlton has established a clear intent focused on both customer and employee wellbeing. The company's 'Gold Standards' are not just about delivering top-tier service to guests; they also ensure that employees, referred to as 'Ladies and Gentlemen', are treated with dignity, respect and care.

Each employee has a clear sense of purpose and is empowered to take ownership of their role, which fosters a sense of pride and responsibility.

An interesting practice at The Ritz-Carlton is the way they encourage open communication and feedback through daily meetings known as 'Line-Ups', where employees from all levels can share their thoughts, challenges and ideas. This consistent dialogue between management and staff ensures that issues related to wellbeing are addressed immediately, promoting an environment of trust and transparency. The result is an organisational culture where employees feel valued and motivated, leading to higher staff retention and exceptional service delivery.

Schools could apply a similar model by holding regular staff check-ins or 'wellbeing briefings', where teachers and support staff can voice concerns or suggestions. By embedding structured, frequent opportunities for staff to engage with leadership, schools can ensure that wellbeing is not just a policy but a lived reality. Empowering teachers to make decisions, whether that's in the classroom or regarding their professional development, can give them the autonomy they need to thrive.

Insights from Teach First

Another example can be drawn from the work of Teach First, a UK-based education charity that emphasises leadership development and staff retention as a core part of their wellbeing strategy. In their schools, they place emphasis on creating a leadership structure that listens to its teachers, providing ongoing support through mentorship programmes and setting realistic expectations around workloads. Their focus on embedding teacher wellbeing as part of their leadership development programme has had measurable effects on teacher retention, which is one of the key indicators of staff wellbeing. Their ability to create a cohesive community where teachers feel heard and respected, and are given the tools to balance work and life is a perfect example of how an intent statement can lead to practical, tangible benefits for an organisation.

Schools looking to develop their own wellbeing intent statement could adapt this by considering mentorship models within their leadership structure. Leaders should ask: How often do we check in with our staff beyond performance reviews? How do we ensure there is space for vulnerability, for staff to express when they are feeling overwhelmed? Setting specific objectives within the intent statement to regularly engage with staff, not just when problems arise but in the continuous ebb and flow of the school year, can help ensure teachers feel genuinely supported.

Insights from Basecamp

A smaller company that offers valuable lessons in staff wellbeing is Basecamp, a project management software company known for its innovative approach to employee wellness. Basecamp has implemented several practices to ensure their employees maintain a healthy work–life balance. They have a strict 40-hour workweek policy and discourage after-hours communication, allowing employees to fully disconnect and recharge.

Basecamp also offers generous benefits, including paid parental leave, sabbaticals and wellness allowances for activities like gym memberships or mental health services. These initiatives demonstrate a commitment to the holistic wellbeing of their staff, leading to high levels of employee satisfaction and retention. All of these initiatives span from a clear intent to support staff wellbeing.

Schools can adapt these practices by setting clear boundaries around work hours and encouraging staff to take time off to recharge. Providing benefits that support physical and mental health can also contribute to a more motivated and satisfied workforce. By examining these diverse examples, from large corporations to smaller businesses, schools can identify and implement strategies that promote staff wellbeing, creating a supportive and thriving educational environment.

Intent as a Living Document

Another key point to emphasise is that an intent statement on wellbeing should not be a static, one-time declaration. It should be a living, breathing document that evolves as the needs of the school community evolve. Much like The Ritz-Carlton's approach, where employee feedback is consistently gathered and acted upon to fine-tune the wellbeing strategy, schools too should be prepared to adapt. Regular reviews and open forums where staff feel comfortable giving feedback on the intent statement itself can help ensure that it stays relevant and impactful. Leaders should see the intent statement as a starting point, one that requires ongoing commitment and active nurturing to grow into something that truly transforms the school's culture.

To sum it up, an intent statement for staff wellbeing isn't a formality. It's a bold and necessary commitment that lays the groundwork for a thriving school environment. When crafted with care and input from all levels of staff, it has the potential to uplift the entire school community, bringing about not only happier, healthier teachers but, ultimately, better outcomes for students. The more intentional a school is in shaping its wellbeing strategy, the more enduring the positive impact will be.

Developing a Policy: The Blueprint for Wellbeing

Intent alone is not enough; it must be translated into tangible policies and practices that shape the daily experiences of staff members. A robust wellbeing policy serves as the cornerstone for nurturing a supportive and thriving school community. One example of how policy, culture and leadership can drive success comes from Bill Walsh, the Hall of Fame coach of the San Francisco 49ers, who transformed the team into a dominant force in the NFL during the 1980s.

Walsh's success didn't stem from raw talent alone – it was about creating a culture where preparation, execution and attention to detail were non-negotiable. He believed that excellence wasn't just a result of athletic prowess but of having the right mindset and structure in place to allow that talent to thrive. His book *The Score Takes Care of Itself: My Philosophy of Leadership* delves deeply into his philosophy, which emphasised the need for setting high standards across every aspect of the organisation, from the way players practised to how support staff contributed to the overall mission. This approach resonates strongly with how schools should think about staff wellbeing – through the lens of setting a clear, actionable policy that enables everyone to perform at their best.

Walsh's principle of 'Standards of Performanc' was central to his success. He didn't just set goals like winning games or championships. Instead, he focused on the small, everyday details: how a player behaved in the locker room, how equipment staff prepared for game day, how the team communicated during pressure situations. His philosophy was that if everyone, from the star quarterback to the administrative assistant, adhered to these exacting standards, the results – wins, championships – would naturally follow.

Schools can adopt a similar mindset when crafting their wellbeing policies. The goal isn't just a vague hope that staff will 'feel supported'. It's about creating specific, actionable practices that ensure every member of staff, from teachers to administrative personnel, operates in an environment where they feel valued and empowered.

For example, a wellbeing policy might detail specific practices such as ensuring staff have access to mental health support, scheduling regular check-ins with leadership and providing structured time for professional development and rest. Just as Walsh meticulously analysed every part of his organisation's operations, schools need to examine all aspects of staff life to ensure that wellbeing is baked into every process. Is there a mechanism for staff to communicate when they feel overwhelmed? Are workloads distributed fairly? Is there an ongoing effort to ensure that staff have time to recharge during the school year, much like Walsh's focus on maintaining the physical and mental stamina of his players throughout a gruelling NFL season?

Another key to Walsh's approach was empowerment. He gave his players – and, by extension, his staff – the freedom to take ownership of their roles. He trusted his team members to adhere to the standards he set, knowing that empowerment leads to accountability. A school wellbeing policy should similarly empower staff by giving them autonomy over certain aspects of their work. Flexible PPA (planning, preparation and assessment) periods, for instance, allow teachers to manage their time more effectively, while mentorship programmes can foster peer-led growth and support.

It's important to note that Walsh's approach wasn't just about controlling every variable. It was about setting a strong framework that gave people the freedom to excel. For example, during games, Walsh encouraged creative problem-solving on the field. He knew that the structure put in place during practice was what enabled players to adapt and thrive in unpredictable situations. Similarly, a wellbeing policy shouldn't be rigid or overly prescriptive. It should provide a framework that supports staff in a variety of ways – whether that's through regular feedback systems, access to counselling or flexible working conditions – but also allow enough flexibility for individual needs and differences. Just as no two players on a football team are the same, no two staff members have identical needs.

Walsh was also a master of continuous improvement. His teams never rested on their laurels; they constantly refined their processes, looking for small ways to get better. Schools can adopt this approach by regularly reviewing and updating their wellbeing policies. Is the current workload distribution still fair? Are staff engagement levels high? Just as Walsh adjusted his playbook week by week, leadership teams in schools should constantly look at how their policies are impacting staff wellbeing and make necessary adjustments. Regular feedback loops, open dialogue and measurable goals should be baked into the policy to ensure that it evolves with the needs of the staff.

In the end, Bill Walsh's philosophy was about creating a culture where every person had a clear sense of their role and how it contributed to the greater good. The same can be said for a school's wellbeing policy. It should be built on the understanding that when staff feel supported, appreciated and empowered, their performance will naturally follow. The 'score' – whether it's student success, staff retention or overall school morale – will take care of itself.

Another powerful example comes from Jeanie Buss, the owner and president of the Los Angeles Lakers. Under her leadership, the Lakers have not only achieved significant success on the court but have also fostered a culture of inclusivity and respect within the organisation. Buss is known for her commitment to creating a supportive environment where every employee feels valued. She has implemented policies that promote open communication, professional development and work–life balance, ensuring that staff wellbeing is a priority.

Buss's approach highlights the importance of leadership in driving a positive organisational culture. By setting clear expectations and providing the necessary support, she has created an environment where staff can thrive. Schools can learn from this by ensuring that their wellbeing policies are not just words on paper but are actively implemented and supported by leadership. This involves regular check-ins with staff, providing opportunities for professional growth and fostering an environment where open communication is encouraged.

Therefore, a wellbeing policy goes beyond mere rhetoric, providing a comprehensive framework that outlines clear objectives, strategies and mechanisms for promoting staff wellbeing.

1. **Workload management:** The wellbeing policy should address the issue of workload management, recognising the importance of maintaining a healthy work–life balance. Specific provisions may include guidelines for reasonable workload expectations, strategies for managing workload during peak periods and mechanisms for monitoring workload distribution to prevent burnout.

2. **Professional development opportunities:** To support staff growth and fulfilment, the policy should emphasise the importance of ongoing professional development. This may involve provisions for access to training and development opportunities, mentoring programmes and sabbatical leave options. Additionally, the policy should encourage a culture of continuous learning and innovation within the school community.
3. **Support and recognition:** Acknowledging the contributions of staff members and providing them with adequate support is essential for fostering a positive work environment. The policy should outline mechanisms for recognising and celebrating staff achievements, such as employee recognition programmes, awards and public commendations. Moreover, it should establish channels for staff support, including access to counselling services, peer support networks and flexible working arrangements.
4. **Inclusive practices:** Recognising the diverse needs of staff members, the policy should incorporate inclusive practices that accommodate various life stages and circumstances. For example, provisions may be included to support staff experiencing menopause, such as access to information, resources and flexible working arrangements to manage symptoms. Additionally, the policy should address leave entitlements for significant personal events, such as attending children's nativity plays or other family obligations, ensuring that staff members feel supported in balancing their professional and personal responsibilities.
5. **Review and evaluation:** To ensure the ongoing effectiveness of the wellbeing policy, regular review and evaluation are essential. The policy should outline processes for soliciting feedback from staff members, assessing the impact of wellbeing initiatives and making necessary adjustments based on evaluation findings. By fostering a culture of continuous improvement, the school can adapt its policies and practices to meet the evolving needs of its staff members, ultimately enhancing overall wellbeing and job satisfaction.

By formalising the school's commitment to staff wellbeing through a comprehensive policy framework, educational leaders demonstrate their dedication to creating a supportive and nurturing work environment where staff members can thrive personally and professionally.

Protocols: The Foundation of Consistency

When implementing a wellbeing policy, the establishment of clear protocols is essential. Protocols provide a structured framework that ensures consistency, fairness and clarity, which are vital in maintaining a supportive and functioning school environment. Without well-defined protocols, even the best intentions can lead to confusion, inefficiency and, ultimately, frustration among staff. In this book, we will explore different protocols in detail, but it is important to understand from the outset why they are crucial for wellbeing initiatives to succeed.

Take the example of flexible PPA, a policy where teachers can take their planning, preparation and assessment time off-site. This is an innovative approach to promoting staff autonomy and improving work–life balance, but without clear protocols, this flexibility can quickly turn into confusion or perceived unfairness. If staff members are unsure about when or how they can take their PPA off-site, or if there are inconsistencies in who is granted this flexibility, resentment may build. Some teachers may feel disadvantaged if they don't have a PPA period at the end of the day, or if the expectations around being reachable during off-site PPA are not clearly communicated.

A well-implemented flexible PPA protocol would include detailed guidelines on when teachers can take their PPA off-site, how to notify their line manager and what expectations exist regarding their availability during that time. For example, staff could be required to log their off-site PPA hours in advance and remain reachable via phone or email. By having these procedures in place, the school creates a system where flexibility is supported but accountability is also maintained. Additionally, protocols should ensure that off-site PPA is equally accessible to all staff, regardless of their timetable.

Without such protocols, staff may face a range of issues:

- **Inconsistency:** Some staff might take PPA off-site without proper notification, while others feel unsure if they are allowed to do so.
- **Unequal access:** Staff with a PPA in the middle of the day may find it impractical to go off-site, while those with PPA at the end of the day may find it easier, leading to feelings of unfairness.
- **Lack of accountability:** If there are no guidelines about how staff should remain contactable or what their off-site work entails, some may feel they are being taken advantage of, while others may feel isolated or unsupported.

This highlights why protocols need to be both comprehensive and flexible, ensuring that everyone knows what is expected while allowing for individual differences. We will come back to flexible PPA later in the book in more detail.

Examples of Where Flexibility Is Important

While protocols provide structure, there are also areas where flexibility is equally important to accommodate the varying needs of staff. For instance, in tech companies like Spotify, flexibility in working hours and remote work has become a cornerstone of their organisational culture. By trusting their employees to manage their time and allowing them to work from wherever they are most productive, Spotify has created a workplace where wellbeing and performance go hand in hand. Schools can learn from this by adopting flexible protocols that consider the diverse needs of staff members while maintaining professional standards.

Another example comes from the world of education: some schools have introduced self-directed professional development days where staff are allowed to choose when and how they complete their development activities. While there are expectations around reporting and outcomes, the flexibility of choosing what fits best into their schedule has led to higher engagement and satisfaction among staff. This balance between structure (protocols) and flexibility (individual choice) can be a model for schools developing wellbeing policies.

Where Protocols Are Non-Negotiable

However, some areas demand strict adherence to protocols. For example, consider safeguarding procedures within schools. Here, flexibility is not an option – there must be strict protocols in place that all staff follow. Every staff member must know how to report concerns, how quickly these concerns should be escalated and the chain of responsibility involved. Without rigid adherence to these protocols, student safety could be compromised.

Similarly, in industries like healthcare, where life-and-death situations are routine, protocols ensure that every member of the team knows exactly what to do in an emergency. In these environments, flexibility around certain decisions is minimal because precision and consistency save lives. Schools, too, have areas where flexibility must be limited, and strict protocols must be followed, such as in student behaviour policies or emergency procedures.

In conclusion, protocols form the bedrock of any effective wellbeing policy. They ensure consistency, fairness and clarity, helping staff understand exactly what is expected of them and what they can expect from the school. However, there must also be a balance between protocols and flexibility, allowing staff to adapt to the unique demands of their roles. Throughout the rest of this book, we will delve deeper into how schools can craft protocols that empower rather than constrain, ensuring that staff wellbeing is both protected and promoted.

Quality Assurance: Making Wellbeing a Reality

While protocols provide the structure for implementing a wellbeing policy, it's quality assurance (QA) that ensures these policies are being consistently applied and delivering the intended impact. Without QA mechanisms in place, even the most well-intentioned wellbeing strategies can fail to have a meaningful effect. Quality assurance allows schools to check that their intent, policy and protocols are aligned and functioning as they should be, while also providing data to inform necessary adjustments.

At its core, QA in a wellbeing context means regularly evaluating how well the policy is being followed, how protocols are being used and whether these efforts are improving the wellbeing of staff as intended. It's an iterative process, where feedback and evidence are used to refine and improve the strategy over time. This is essential because staff wellbeing is not static – it changes as new challenges emerge, whether through shifting workloads, changing team dynamics or external pressures.

Aligning Intent, Policy and Protocols

The first step in quality assurance is to ensure alignment between the wellbeing intent, the policy framework and the protocols in place. Let's take the example of flexible PPA: the intent may be to offer staff autonomy in managing their workload, improving both their professional performance and personal wellbeing. The policy formalises this, outlining who can take their PPA off-site and under what conditions, while the protocols detail the day-to-day operational procedures staff must follow.

To evaluate whether the intent, policy and protocols are aligned, school leaders should ask the following questions:

- Is the intent clear and actionable within the policy?
- Does the policy contain mechanisms that make the intent achievable?
- Are the protocols enabling staff to use the policy effectively, without creating confusion or inconsistency?

In practice, this can involve gathering regular feedback from staff who are using the flexible PPA option. Are they finding it beneficial? Do they understand the protocols? Is the policy being applied fairly across different departments? By checking this alignment regularly, schools can ensure that their efforts to improve wellbeing are both meaningful and sustainable.

Evidence-Based Quality Assurance

The importance of quality assurance is well supported by research. A study conducted by the University of Warwick found that organisations with structured QA processes had better employee satisfaction and performance outcomes than those without such frameworks. Specifically, the study highlighted that regular evaluations and adjustments based on feedback increased employee engagement by up to 20 per cent over time (Oswald et al., 2015). Furthermore, a report by the Chartered Institute of Personnel and Development (CIPD, 2016) emphasises that organisations that prioritise QA not only enhance employee engagement but also experience reduced turnover rates and improved overall performance.

Similarly, in the education sector, a study by Gibbs and Coffey (2004) on the effectiveness of teaching development programmes showed that continuous feedback and evaluation were critical in improving the quality of teaching. This research underscores the value of QA in maintaining alignment between a school's wellbeing intent and its practical implementation. Additionally, the work of Hattie and Timperley (2007) highlights the role of feedback as a fundamental component of effective teaching and learning. Their meta-analysis indicates that feedback can increase learning outcomes by up to 30 per cent, showcasing how structured QA processes can lead to significant improvements in educational contexts.

Moreover, the integration of QA mechanisms in educational settings promotes a culture of continuous improvement. A study by Stiggins and Chappuis (2005) reveals that effective assessment practices, which are a key aspect of QA, not only support student learning but also enhance teachers' professional development by fostering reflective practice. This cycle of feedback and improvement is essential for aligning educational practices with desired wellbeing outcomes.

Methods of Quality Assurance in Schools

In schools, quality assurance can take multiple forms. One common approach is to use staff wellbeing surveys as a regular touchpoint to measure the overall climate of wellbeing. These surveys can be conducted quarterly or biannually, depending on the size of the school and the complexity of the wellbeing initiatives in place. Surveys are useful for gathering broad quantitative data, but they need to be supplemented by qualitative methods such as focus groups or one-on-one interviews to gain a deeper understanding of staff experiences.

In addition to surveys, peer reviews can be an effective QA tool. For example, leadership teams from different departments could conduct reciprocal reviews of each other's adherence to wellbeing protocols. This helps in identifying any discrepancies or inconsistencies in how the policy is applied. Peer reviews also encourage accountability and foster a sense of collective responsibility for wellbeing across the entire staff.

The Role of Data in Quality Assurance

Data plays a crucial role in ensuring that the school's wellbeing strategies are working as intended. For instance, if a school introduces flexible PPA as a wellbeing initiative, data collection should include:

- How many staff members are utilising the flexible PPA policy?
- Are certain departments using it more than others, and why?
- Is there a measurable impact on staff absenteeism, stress levels or job satisfaction?

Schools can track these data points over time to assess whether the flexible PPA policy is having the desired effect. If the data shows that only a small percentage of staff are using the policy, it may indicate that the protocols are too restrictive or that there is a lack of clarity about how to use the policy. Conversely, if absenteeism or reported stress levels drop after the introduction of flexible PPA, this would provide evidence that the initiative is working.

A case study from the NHS demonstrates the power of using data in quality assurance for staff wellbeing. The NHS has implemented a comprehensive staff wellbeing programme across various trusts, including mental health support and flexible working options. By regularly measuring staff satisfaction, mental health scores and absenteeism rates, the NHS has been able to adjust its policies in real time. Over the course of five years, this data-driven approach led to a reduction in absenteeism and an increase in staff retention, particularly in high-pressure departments such as emergency care (West et al., 2015).

The Pitfalls of Skipping Quality Assurance

Without robust QA mechanisms in place, schools risk undermining their own wellbeing initiatives. For instance, a cover card policy that allows staff to take an hour off as needed throughout the year may be introduced with the best intentions. However, without proper monitoring and evaluation, this policy could backfire. Staff members might feel that their colleagues are abusing the system, leading to perceptions of unfairness or preferential treatment. Such feelings can foster resentment, particularly if some staff members frequently utilise their cover cards while others do not, resulting in an imbalance in workload and increased pressure on those left to manage classroom responsibilities. Over time, this could lead to declining morale, as staff may feel unsupported and overwhelmed by their additional responsibilities.

Moreover, if the cover card policy is not clearly communicated, confusion can arise regarding when it is appropriate to use it. This ambiguity may lead to further dissatisfaction among staff, as they may feel uncertain about their rights and responsibilities. By contrast, when QA mechanisms are effectively employed, schools can assess how such policies impact overall staff wellbeing and satisfaction. Regular evaluations can uncover any issues that might not have been apparent at the outset, enabling the school to address them proactively. If QA assessments reveal that the cover card policy is indeed causing strain in specific areas – such as increased workload for colleagues covering classes – adjustments can be made to the policy. This might include clarifying the conditions under which cover cards can be used, ensuring equitable distribution of cover responsibilities or providing additional resources and support for staff.

Quality assurance is not about rigidly enforcing rules; rather, it is about ensuring that the school's intent, policy and protocols are all aligned and functioning harmoniously. Through an ongoing QA process, schools can create a feedback loop that not only identifies areas for improvement but also allows for the adaptation of wellbeing strategies based on real-time data and staff input. This iterative process enables schools to refine their initiatives continuously, ensuring that staff feel supported, valued and empowered in their roles. When staff know that their wellbeing is a priority, they are more likely to engage positively with the school community, ultimately leading to enhanced educational outcomes for students. By investing in quality assurance, schools can create a culture of trust and collaboration that fosters a thriving work environment.

By regularly evaluating the clarity and actionability of wellbeing intents, gathering comprehensive data, conducting frequent surveys and addressing potential risks, schools can create an environment where staff feel valued and empowered. This commitment to continuous improvement and quality assurance is essential for fostering a positive culture that prioritises the wellbeing of all staff members.

Conclusion

Creating a culture of staff wellbeing is a multifaceted endeavour that requires intentional structural design. The examples from sports, business and education illustrate that successful wellbeing initiatives are deeply embedded in the fabric of the organisation. Whether it's a café at Paris Saint-Germain, Google's micro-kitchens or a school's protected time, these structures foster connection, collaboration and support. They are not just physical spaces but symbolic representations of the values and priorities of the organisation.

As a leader, it is crucial to examine and redesign the spaces and systems within your organisation to align with the culture you aim to build. Small, purposeful changes can have a significant impact on staff morale and cohesion. By prioritising staff wellbeing through thoughtful structural design, you create an environment where everyone can thrive. This approach not only enhances individual wellbeing but also drives collective success and innovation, setting the stage for a positive and supportive organisational culture.

Reflective Questions

1. How clear and actionable is our wellbeing intent within our current policies, and do our protocols enable staff to use these policies effectively?
2. How do we currently evaluate the effectiveness of our wellbeing initiatives, and what methods do we use to gather both quantitative and qualitative data on staff wellbeing?
3. How frequently do we conduct staff wellbeing surveys, and what insights have we gained from them to foster a sense of collective responsibility for wellbeing?
4. What specific data points do we track to assess the impact of our wellbeing initiatives, and how do we use this data to identify areas for improvement?
5. What potential risks do we face if we do not have robust quality assurance mechanisms in place for our wellbeing initiatives, and how do we address perceptions of unfairness or preferential treatment that may arise?

Reflecting on these questions can help school leaders ensure that their wellbeing policies and protocols are effectively aligned with their intent, leading to a supportive and thriving school community.

References and Further Reading

Ancelotti, C. (2016). *Quiet Leadership: Winning Hearts, Minds and Matches*. Penguin Random House.
Bock, L. (2015). *Work Rules! Insights from Inside Google That Will Transform How You Live and Lead*. Twelve.
Chartered Institute of Personnel and Development (CIPD). (2016). *Employee Engagement: Driving Organisational Performance*. London: CIPD.
Desimone, L. M., & Pak, K. (2017). 'Instructional Coaching as High-Quality Professional Development.' *Theory Into Practice*, 56(1), 3–12.

Duhigg, C. (2016). *Smarter Faster Better: The Secrets of Being Productive*. Random House.
Education Support. (2021). 'Teacher Wellbeing Index 2021.' Education Support. www.educationsupport.org.uk/media/qzna4gxb/twix-2021.pdf
Fullan, M. (2014). *The Principal: Three Keys to Maximizing Impact*. Jossey-Bass.
Gibbs, G., & Coffey, M. (2004). 'The Impact of Training of University Teachers on Their Teaching Skills, Their Approach to Teaching and the Approach to Learning of Their Students.' *Active Learning in Higher Education, 5*(1), 87–100.
Hargreaves, A., & O'Connor, M. T. (2018). *Collaborative Professionalism: When Teaching Together Means Learning for All*. Corwin.
Hattie, J., & Timperley, H. (2007). 'The Power of Feedback.' *Review of Educational Research, 77*(1), 81–112.
Ingersoll, R., & Strong, M. (2011). 'The Impact of Induction and Mentoring Programs for Beginning Teachers: A Critical Review of the Research.' *Review of Educational Research, 81*(2), 201–233.
Maslach, C., & Leiter, M. P. (2016). *Burnout at Work: Causes and Cures*. Psychology Press.
Michelli, J. A. (2008). *The New Gold Standard: 5 Leadership Principles for Creating a Legendary Customer Experience Courtesy of The Ritz-Carlton Hotel Company*. McGraw-Hill Education.
Oswald, A. J., Proto, E., & Sgroi, D. (2015). 'Happiness and Productivity.' *Journal of Labor Economics, 33*(4), 789–822.
Sims, S. (2017). *Tackling Teacher Retention: What Teach First Does Right*. National Foundation for Educational Research.
Stiggins, R., & Chappuis, J. (2005). 'Using Student-Involved Classroom Assessment to Close Achievement Gaps.' *Theory Into Practice, 44*(1), 11–18.
The Ritz-Carlton Leadership Center. (n.d.). Building Strong Relationships. Retrieved from https://ritzcarltonleadershipcenter.com
Viac, C., & Fraser, P. (2020). 'Teacher Wellbeing: A Framework for Data Collection and Analysis.' OECD Education Working Papers, No. 213. OECD Publishing. www.oecd.org/content/dam/oecd/en/publications/reports/2020/01/teachers-well-being_bdafdeaf/c36fc9d3-en.pdf
Walsh, B., Jamison, S., & Walsh, C. (2009). *The Score Takes Care of Itself: My Philosophy of Leadership*. Portfolio.
West, M., Dawson, J., & Kaur, M. (2015). *NHS Staff Management and Health Service Quality: Results from the NHS Staff Survey and Related Data*. The King's Fund.

Chapter 3
Leading

As leaders, it is important that we take an active role in promoting and supporting mental health within our organisations. In this chapter, we will explore how leaders from various industries, including sports and business, can provide guidance and inspiration for leaders in schools who are working to improve the mental health of their staff and students.

Leaders in sports, for example, often have to manage the physical and mental wellbeing of their athletes in high-pressure and high-stress environments. These leaders have valuable experience in recognising the signs of stress and burnout, and in providing support and resources to their teams. In the same way, business leaders have to handle the challenges of the workforce and create a positive work environment for their employees.

In addition to sharing examples from these industries, we will also examine the ways in which educational leaders can create and promote a positive and supportive school culture. This can include implementing policies and programmes that promote mental health and wellbeing, fostering open and honest communication, and providing opportunities for professional development and support for staff.

Furthermore, we will discuss the importance of creating an inclusive environment that is sensitive to the diverse needs of students and staff, and how leaders can promote and support the wellbeing of those who are marginalised or at risk.

Insights from Indra Nooyi

Indra Nooyi, the former CEO of PepsiCo, provides a compelling example of how leadership can effectively manage teams and organisations while prioritising staff wellbeing. Nooyi's tenure at PepsiCo was marked by her commitment to creating a healthy and positive environment for employees, which can be particularly relevant for leaders in the education sector.

Nooyi's leadership philosophy was built on the principle of 'Performance with Purpose', which emphasised the importance of delivering strong financial results while also making a positive impact on society and the environment. She believed that a company's success was intrinsically linked to the wellbeing of its employees. This approach resonates strongly with how schools should think about staff wellbeing – through the lens of setting a clear, actionable policy that enables everyone to perform at their best.

One key aspect of Nooyi's leadership was her focus on communication and transparency. She regularly engaged with employees at all levels of the organisation, encouraging open and honest dialogue. This practice helped create an atmosphere where employees felt comfortable expressing their ideas and concerns, which is crucial for addressing sensitive issues related to mental health and wellbeing.

Nooyi also placed a strong emphasis on diversity and inclusion, recognising that a diverse workforce brings a variety of perspectives and ideas that drive innovation. She implemented policies that promoted gender equality and supported the professional development of women within the company. This inclusive approach can be particularly relevant for leaders in education, as fostering a diverse and supportive environment can have a direct impact on the mental health and wellbeing of staff.

Furthermore, Nooyi understood the importance of work–life balance and implemented initiatives to support employees in managing their personal and professional lives. She introduced flexible working arrangements and wellness programmes that encouraged employees to take care of their physical and mental health. Schools can adopt similar practices by providing flexible working options and promoting a culture of wellbeing that supports staff in achieving a healthy work–life balance.

Indra Nooyi's leadership at PepsiCo provides valuable insights into how leaders can create a positive and supportive organisational culture. By prioritising communication, diversity and work–life balance, educational leaders can foster an environment where staff feel valued and empowered, ultimately enhancing the overall success of the institution.

Takeaway

Indra Nooyi's leadership at PepsiCo offers powerful lessons for schools focusing on staff wellbeing. Her principle of 'Performance with Purpose' underscores the importance of linking staff wellbeing to overall success through clear, actionable policies. Nooyi's emphasis on communication and transparency highlights the need for school leaders to engage regularly with staff, fostering an environment where ideas and concerns can be openly discussed. Her commitment to diversity and inclusion demonstrates how promoting equality and supporting professional development can enhance staff wellbeing. Additionally, Nooyi's focus on work–life balance through flexible working arrangements and wellness programmes shows that schools can support staff in managing their personal and professional lives, leading to a healthier work–life balance.

Insights from Carlo Ancelotti

Carlo Ancelotti's book *Quiet Leadership* provides insights on how leaders can effectively manage teams and organisations. One key theme of his book is the importance of creating a healthy and positive environment for team members, which can be particularly relevant for leaders in the education sector, where the wellbeing of students and staff is a top priority.

In *Quiet Leadership*, Ancelotti writes, 'Creating a positive environment is crucial for mental and emotional well-being and for getting the best out of people' (2016, p. 71). He stresses the importance of a leader being able to 'sense the emotional state of their players' (p. 74) and being 'attentive to the needs of their team' (p. 75). By understanding the emotional and mental wellbeing of their team members, leaders can take the necessary steps to address any issues and create a positive and supportive environment.

Ancelotti also emphasises the importance of communication in leadership, writing, 'Good communication is crucial for any team, especially when dealing with sensitive issues like mental health' (p. 120). He suggests that leaders should 'encourage open and honest dialogue' (p. 121) and 'create an atmosphere where people feel comfortable expressing their feelings' (p. 122). This can help team members feel heard and supported, which is particularly important when dealing with sensitive issues related to mental health.

In addition, Ancelotti recommends 'acknowledging and understanding the different personalities and temperaments on your team' (p. 150). By being able to understand the unique needs and characteristics of each team member, leaders can create a more inclusive and supportive environment.

Takeaway

Carlo Ancelotti's *Quiet Leadership* offers valuable lessons for school leaders focusing on staff wellbeing. His emphasis on creating a healthy and positive environment underscores the importance of understanding the emotional and mental wellbeing of team members. By being attentive to the needs of staff, leaders can address issues proactively and foster a supportive atmosphere. Ancelotti's focus on good communication highlights the need for open and honest dialogue, which is crucial for dealing with sensitive mental health issues. Encouraging staff to express their feelings can help them feel heard and supported. Additionally, acknowledging and understanding the different personalities and temperaments within the team can lead to a more inclusive and supportive environment. By adopting these principles, school leaders can create a culture where staff wellbeing is prioritised, ultimately enhancing the overall success of the institution.

Insights from Alex Ferguson

In a similar vein, Alex Ferguson's book *Leading* provides insight into the leadership style and strategies that he used during his successful tenure as manager of Manchester United Football Club. While the book primarily focuses on leadership in the sports industry, it can also provide valuable guidance for leaders in other industries, including education.

One key theme in the book is the importance of creating a positive and supportive culture within an organisation. In *Leading*, Ferguson writes, 'A positive culture creates energy and a determination to succeed' (Ferguson & Moritz, 2015, p. 73). He emphasises the importance of setting high standards and expectations for team members, while also providing the support and resources they need to meet those expectations. This can be particularly relevant for leaders in the education sector, who are responsible for creating a positive and supportive learning environment for students and staff.

Ferguson also stresses the importance of clear and effective communication in leadership. He writes that 'communication is critical in any organisation' (p. 148) and suggests that leaders should be 'constantly engaging with your team to understand their views, to listen to their feedback, and to give them your perspective' (p. 149). This can be particularly important for leaders in schools, as clear and effective communication can help promote a positive and supportive school culture, and address sensitive issues related to mental health.

Another key leadership strategy discussed in *Leading* is the importance of creating an inclusive environment that values diversity and recognises the unique strengths and contributions of each team member. Ferguson writes, 'It's important to create a culture in which everyone feels valued and respected' (p. 215). He also emphasises the importance of being aware of and responsive to the needs of all team members, including those who may be marginalised or at risk. By fostering an inclusive environment, leaders in education can help promote the mental health and wellbeing of students and staff.

Alex Ferguson's book *Leading* provides valuable guidance for leaders in education looking to create a positive and supportive school culture, while promoting the mental health and wellbeing of students and staff. By setting high standards, fostering clear and effective communication, and creating an inclusive environment, educational leaders can help promote a positive culture within their schools.

Takeaway

Alex Ferguson's *Leading* provides essential lessons for school leaders aiming to enhance staff wellbeing. His focus on cultivating a positive and supportive culture underscores the necessity of setting high standards while ensuring staff have the resources and support needed to achieve them. Ferguson's emphasis on effective communication highlights the importance of regular engagement with staff, fostering an environment where feedback is actively sought and valued. Additionally, his dedication to creating an inclusive environment that appreciates diversity and recognises the unique contributions of each team member is vital for promoting mental health and wellbeing. By integrating these principles, educational leaders can build a school culture where staff feel appreciated, respected and empowered, ultimately driving the institution's success.

Insights from James Kerr

Building upon the insights gleaned from Alex Ferguson's book on leadership, James Kerr's *Legacy: What the All Blacks Can Teach Us About the Business of Life* offers a compelling exploration of leadership and team culture, as demonstrated by the New Zealand All Blacks rugby team. While Kerr's book predominantly examines leadership within the sports realm, its lessons extend far beyond, resonating with leaders across various industries, including education. Particularly noteworthy is its relevance to mental health considerations, shedding light on strategies to foster a supportive and resilient organisational culture.

One key theme in the book is the importance of creating a strong and positive team culture. Kerr writes, 'The culture of a team or organisation is the glue that binds it together. It's the environment in which the team functions and the expectations that drive it' (2013, p. 44). He emphasises the importance of promoting a culture of excellence and accountability, while also fostering a sense of belonging and unity among team members. This can be particularly relevant for leaders in the education sector, as a positive culture can have a direct impact on the mental health and wellbeing of students and staff.

In *Legacy*, Kerr also emphasises the importance of creating an inclusive and diverse environment that values the unique strengths and contributions of each team member. He writes, 'The power of diversity is that it brings different perspectives and ideas to the table' (p. 181). This is particularly important for leaders in schools, as a diverse and inclusive environment can promote a sense of belonging and can also help to reduce stress and anxiety that some students may experience due to feeling marginalised or not accepted.

Another key leadership strategy discussed in *Legacy* is the importance of clear and effective communication within a team, specifically when it comes to sensitive topics such as mental health. Kerr writes, 'Communication is a key component of any successful team' (p. 105) and suggests that leaders should 'create an environment where people feel comfortable giving feedback and sharing ideas' (p. 110). By providing opportunities for open and honest communication, leaders in education can help to break down the stigmas surrounding mental health and create a culture of openness and support.

Takeaway

James Kerr's *Legacy* offers profound lessons for school leaders dedicated to staff wellbeing. The book underscores the significance of cultivating a cohesive and positive team culture, which serves as the foundation for mental health and overall wellbeing. Kerr highlights the power of diversity, advocating for an environment that values each individual's unique strengths and contributions. This inclusive approach can help reduce feelings of marginalisation and foster a sense of belonging among staff. Furthermore, Kerr emphasises the critical role of communication, particularly in addressing sensitive issues like mental health. By creating a space where open and honest dialogue is encouraged, school leaders can dismantle stigma and build a supportive community. Embracing these principles can enable educational leaders to create a resilient and nurturing environment, ultimately enhancing the wellbeing and performance of their staff.

Insights from Sara Blakely

Expanding our exploration of leadership literature beyond the sports realm, the leadership principles and practices at Spanx, founded by Sara Blakely, offer valuable insights. Spanx is renowned for its innovation and success in the fashion industry. While the principles discussed here are rooted in business, they are highly adaptable and applicable across diverse industries, including education. One pivotal theme in Blakely's leadership is the importance of creating a culture of experimentation and innovation. Sara Blakely emphasised the importance of encouraging creativity, taking risks and learning from failures. This can be particularly relevant for leaders in the education sector, who are responsible for creating a positive and supportive learning environment for students and staff. For example, how many schools provide their middle leaders with a budget to support their team's wellbeing? Very few. This shows where innovation, as expressed at Spanx, can shift cultures.

Blakely also stresses the importance of effective communication and transparency within an organisation. She believes that transparency and open communication are essential to building trust and alignment within an organisation. She created an environment where people could speak their minds freely. This can be particularly important for leaders in schools, as clear and effective communication can help promote a positive and supportive school culture, and address sensitive issues related to mental health. Reflect on your own school or setting. How do you create feedback loops where people can express their feelings? Can you create town-hall-style meetings to facilitate conversation? There are invariably issues with this, as they can become forums to complain. However, by implementing structured feedback mechanisms and fostering an environment of open dialogue, leaders can mitigate these challenges and cultivate a culture of constructive communication. Town-hall-style meetings can serve as valuable platforms for facilitating conversations and soliciting input from staff, students and stakeholders. Additionally, establishing anonymous feedback channels, such as suggestion boxes or online surveys, can provide individuals with a safe space to express their thoughts and concerns without fear of repercussion. Moreover, leaders should actively listen to feedback, acknowledge perspectives and take appropriate action to address issues raised. By prioritising transparency and communication, leaders can foster trust, enhance morale and create a more inclusive and supportive school community.

Another key leadership strategy discussed by Blakely is the importance of creating a customer-centric culture. Blakely's leadership was customer-centric, always putting the customer first. This can be particularly relevant for leaders in education, as a customer-centric approach can help leaders in education to focus on the needs and wellbeing of students, and to create a positive and supportive learning environment for them. In alignment with the customer-centric approach advocated by Blakely, educational leaders should view students entering mental health support systems as valued customers, prioritising their experiences and wellbeing over organisational structural barriers. By adopting this perspective, leaders can shift their focus towards understanding and addressing the unique needs of each student, fostering a culture of empathy, support and inclusivity within the school community. Just as Spanx places the customer at the forefront of its operations, educational leaders can prioritise student-centric policies and initiatives that enhance the overall learning experience and promote positive mental health outcomes. By embracing a customer-centric mindset, leaders can cultivate a learning environment where students feel valued, supported and empowered to thrive academically, socially and emotionally.

The above approach may initially seem uncomfortable for schools accustomed to traditional hierarchical structures and bureaucratic processes. However, it is imperative for educational leaders to recognise that prioritising staff and students' needs and wellbeing is at the heart of their mission. This shift in perspective not only enhances the educational experience but also fosters a sense of belonging and empowerment among students and staff, ultimately contributing to their overall wellbeing and academic success. While challenging, adopting a customer-centric approach is essential for schools to adapt to the evolving needs of students and staff, and prepare them for success in an increasingly complex and interconnected world.

Takeaway

Sara Blakely's leadership at Spanx offers transformative insights for school leaders focused on staff wellbeing. Her emphasis on fostering a culture of experimentation and innovation highlights the importance of encouraging creativity and risk-taking within educational settings. By supporting innovative practices, schools can create environments where staff feel empowered to explore new ideas and approaches. Blakely's commitment to effective communication and transparency underscores the need for open dialogue and trust within schools. Establishing structured feedback mechanisms and promoting honest conversations can help address sensitive issues related to mental health and build a supportive community. Additionally, Blakely's customer-centric approach, which prioritises the needs and experiences of customers, can be adapted by educational leaders to focus on the wellbeing of students and staff. Viewing staff as valued members of the school community and prioritising their wellbeing can foster a culture of empathy and support. By embracing these principles, school leaders can create a nurturing and inclusive environment that enhances the overall wellbeing and performance of their staff.

 ## Insights from Simon Sinek

Delving into the principles expounded by Simon Sinek in *Start with Why* (2009), educational leaders can unlock a profound shift in their strategic approach to mental health within schools. By anchoring their endeavours in the fundamental question of 'why', leaders can challenge old and established paradigms, paving the way for innovative solutions and transformative change. This philosophical framework encourages leaders to interrogate the underlying motivations and aspirations behind their mental health initiatives, enabling them to cultivate a deeper understanding of the purpose and significance of their efforts.

Incorporating the 'why' into mental health strategic thinking fosters a holistic approach that transcends conventional wisdom. Rather than merely focusing on the 'what' and 'how' of mental health support, leaders are prompted to explore the underlying motivations driving their actions. This introspective process encourages leaders to question entrenched practices and consider alternative approaches that align more closely with the core values and objectives of their school community.

One such alternative approach may involve re-evaluating traditional mentoring practices within schools. Instead of adhering to rigid structures and pre-defined outcomes, leaders can embrace unstructured mentoring as a means of fostering authentic connections and meaningful interactions between staff and students. In this context, mentoring sessions serve as opportunities for genuine dialogue and mutual support, where staff members engage with students in candid conversations without the pressure of predefined agendas. By shifting the focus from outcomes to relationships, unstructured mentoring creates space for organic growth and personal development, empowering students to navigate their mental health journey with confidence and resilience.

In essence, integrating the 'why' into mental health strategic thinking empowers educational leaders to challenge the status quo and embrace innovative approaches that prioritise the wellbeing and flourishing of students. By fostering a culture of curiosity, exploration and authenticity, leaders can cultivate a learning environment where mental health support is not merely a programme or initiative but a fundamental ethos that permeates every aspect of school life.

One key concept in the book is the idea that people are not inspired by what an organisation does but rather by why it does it. In the case of a school, this means that students are not just motivated by the curriculum and coursework, but by the underlying purpose and mission of the school. As Sinek writes, 'The goal is not just to sell to people who need what you have, but to sell to people who believe what you believe" (2009, p. 25). In the context of mental health, this means that leaders need to communicate not just the programmes and services available to support students' mental health but also the school's values and belief in the importance of mental health.

Another key concept in the book is the idea of the 'golden circle', which consists of three parts: the 'why', the 'how' and the 'what'. Sinek argues that most organisations start with the 'what' (i.e. the products or services they offer) and then work backwards to the 'why' (i.e. their purpose or belief). However, the most successful organisations start with the 'why' and then work outward to the 'how' and 'what'. In the case of a school, this means starting with the 'why' of promoting mental health and wellbeing, and then working out to the specific programmes and services that are offered. Sinek writes, 'When you start with why, you have a foundation, a principle, a belief that you can build on, a north star that guides everything else' (p. 17).

Takeaway

To implement the ideas from *Start with Why* in the context of mental health in schools, leaders can do the following:

- Clearly communicate the school's values and belief in the importance of mental health and wellbeing. It should be referenced in the curriculum intent statement of the school (more of which later).
- Use language that reflects these values and beliefs when discussing mental health and related programmes and services. This should be captured in the policies and protocols.
- Start with the 'why' of promoting mental health and wellbeing and use that as a foundation for all decisions related to mental health support.
- Encourage open and honest conversation in the community about mental health and wellbeing, and actively work to remove any stigmas or biases that may discourage individuals from seeking support.

Insights from John Adair

Effective Leadership by John Adair (2009) offers invaluable insights tailored specifically for leaders seeking to enhance staff mental health and wellbeing within their organisations. Renowned as a leading authority in leadership studies, Adair provides a comprehensive roadmap for navigating the complexities of leadership, with a particular emphasis on fostering a supportive and conducive environment for staff wellbeing.

At the heart of Adair's approach lies a deep understanding of the interplay between task, team and individual dynamics within leadership. He contends that effective leaders must skilfully balance these elements, adapting their leadership styles to suit diverse circumstances. Recognising the significance of self-awareness, Adair advocates for leaders to identify their own strengths and weaknesses, thereby equipping themselves to excel in various leadership roles.

Central to Adair's teachings is the imperative of clear communication and goal-setting in leadership practices. He underscores that effective leadership hinges on the ability to articulate a compelling vision and inspire others to align with it. Moreover, Adair underscores the importance of meticulous planning and decisive decision-making, asserting that leaders must possess the acumen to guide their teams towards shared objectives.

Takeaway

In essence, *Effective Leadership* isn't just another leadership manual – it's a compass for leaders who truly care about the mental health and wellbeing of their staff. Through Adair's wisdom, leaders can tap into a more authentic style, one that prioritises empathy, communication and empowerment. By weaving these principles into the fabric of their organisation, leaders create a nurturing environment where every team member feels valued, supported and inspired to bring their best selves to work every day.

 ## Insights from James Clear

In the realm of fostering mental health among staff in schools, *Atomic Habits: An Easy & Proven Way to Build Good Habits & Break Bad Ones* by James Clear (2018) offers invaluable insights. Clear's self-help book delves into the transformative power of small, incremental changes in behaviour, highlighting the concept of 'atomic habits' – tiny adjustments that can lead to significant improvements over time. By emphasising the significance of cultivating these manageable habits, Clear provides a practical roadmap for educators to enhance their overall wellbeing and resilience.

One key concept in the book is the idea of 'habit stacking', which involves linking new habits to existing ones in order to make them easier to establish. For example, Clear suggests that if someone wants to start exercising more, they could link their new habit of going for a run to their existing habit of drinking coffee in the morning. By associating the new habit with something that they already do on a regular basis, it becomes more likely that they will stick with it.

Another important idea in the book is the concept of 'identity-based habits', which involve aligning one's habits with their sense of self. Clear argues that people are more likely to stick with a habit if they see it as being in line with who they are and what they stand for. Some examples of what this looks like are provided below.

Habit Stacking and Identity-Based Habits for Staff Wellbeing

- **Habit stacking:** Link new behaviours with existing routines to establish and maintain healthy habits.
  - Incorporate short mindfulness exercises into daily routines, such as deep breathing during prep periods.
- **Identity-based habits:** Align behaviours with one's sense of self to reinforce positive self-perception and promote sustainable change.
  - Frame self-care as an essential aspect of being a caring and dedicated educator, making activities like exercise, meditation or journaling integral to the educator's identity.
- **Acts of kindness:** Use habit stacking to incorporate small acts of kindness and appreciation into daily interactions.
  - Link expressions of gratitude or encouragement to routine activities like staff meetings or collaborative planning sessions to foster a culture of support and camaraderie.
- **Cultural emphasis:** Create a culture of identity-based habits by emphasising the importance of self-care and mental wellbeing.
  - Frame healthy habits such as exercise, sleep and mindfulness as aligned with the school's values and mission, encouraging regular practice among students and staff.

Takeaway

Overall, *Atomic Habits* provides a powerful framework for making small changes that can have a big impact on overall wellbeing and success. By understanding the science of habit formation and applying the concepts of habit stacking and identity-based habits, we can help students and staff to create healthy habits that will serve them well in the long term.

Insights from Carol Dweck

Mindset: The New Psychology of Success by Carol S. Dweck is a self-help and psychology book that explores the concept of 'growth mindset' and its impact on personal and professional development. The book was first published in 2006.

In the book, Dweck defines growth mindset as 'the belief that one's abilities and intelligence can be developed through dedication and hard work' (2006, p. 7). She contrasts this with a 'fixed mindset', which is the belief that one's abilities are predetermined and cannot be changed. Dweck argues that having a growth mindset is crucial for achieving success in all areas of life.

One key idea in the book is that praising someone for their innate abilities (such as intelligence) can lead to a fixed mindset, while praising someone for their efforts and hard work can lead to a growth mindset. Dweck writes, 'Praising children's intelligence harms their motivation and it harms their performance' (p. 39).

Another important concept in the book is that of 'challenge-seeking'. Dweck argues that people with a growth mindset actively seek out challenges and view them as opportunities for growth, while those with a fixed mindset tend to avoid challenges and view them as threats to their abilities.

In the context of student and staff mental health in schools, the concept of growth mindset can be applied in a number of ways. For example, teachers could use growth mindset language when giving feedback to students and praising them for their effort and progress. This could help to promote a positive attitude towards learning and increase students' motivation to succeed.

Additionally, schools could work to create a culture of growth mindset by emphasising the importance of effort, perseverance and continuous learning. By framing failure and challenges as opportunities for growth and development, students and staff may be more likely to approach them with a positive attitude and a willingness to learn from their mistakes.

Takeaway

Mindset: The New Psychology of Success by Carol Dweck might seem like old hat in education, but its principles still pack a punch. The concept of a growth mindset – believing that abilities can be developed through dedication and hard work – remains a game-changer. For schools, this means fostering an environment where both students and staff are encouraged to embrace challenges, learn from criticism and persist in the face of setbacks. By embedding a growth mindset into the school culture, leaders can inspire a more resilient, motivated and high-performing community. It's not just about student success; it's about creating a thriving ecosystem where everyone, from teachers to administrators, believes in their potential to grow and excel.

Conclusion

In this chapter, we've delved into the profound impact that leadership can have on the wellbeing of staff, drawing inspiration from both the educational sphere and other sectors such as sports and business. Leaders like Sara Blakely, the founder of Spanx, have shown that resilience and innovation can drive success even in the face of initial setbacks. Similarly, Indra Nooyi, the former CEO of PepsiCo, exemplifies how compassionate leadership and strategic vision can transform an organisation. From the world of sports, Alex Ferguson's tenure at Manchester United highlights the importance of fostering a strong team culture and valuing each member's contribution. Simon Sinek's insights on leadership emphasise the significance of starting with a clear purpose and building trust within teams.

The insights gained from these leaders and writers provide a broad perspective on the critical role school leaders play in actively fostering an environment that promotes mental and emotional wellbeing. The key takeaway is that wellbeing initiatives are not about isolated programmes or strategies, but rather about building a sustained culture of support, transparency and innovation.

Creating a positive school culture, much like creating a high-functioning sports team or a successful business, requires intentional leadership, clear communication and a deep understanding of the needs of individuals. By fostering an environment of trust, openness and inclusivity, educational leaders can ensure that staff feel valued and empowered. These strategies not only benefit the individuals but enhance the overall effectiveness of the organisation, allowing staff to thrive in their roles and students to benefit from a more supportive learning environment.

It's essential to recognise that leaders cannot be all things to all people. They are fallible, and failing in creating the right culture is a natural part of the leadership journey. What truly matters is the commitment to continuous improvement. As Sara Blakely once noted, embracing failure as a learning opportunity is crucial for growth. Indra Nooyi's tenure at PepsiCo was marked by her willingness to adapt and innovate, even when faced with significant challenges. Alex Ferguson's success was built on his ability to reflect on setbacks and continuously refine his approach. Simon Sinek's philosophy underscores the importance of leaders being open to feedback and willing to evolve.

In the realm of education, leaders like Imogen Senior, a headteacher with over two decades of experience, exemplify the power of dedicated and empathetic leadership. Imogen has been instrumental in transforming her school's culture by prioritising the mental and emotional wellbeing of both staff and students. Her journey, marked by resilience and a commitment to inclusivity, highlights the significant impact that leaders can have in education. Despite the challenges and barriers that women often face in leadership roles, Imogen's story is a testament to the positive changes that can be achieved through perseverance and a focus on creating a supportive environment.

The success of any wellbeing initiative lies in continuous reflection and adaptation. Quality assurance mechanisms are vital in ensuring that policies and practices are aligned with the needs of staff. Regular feedback, open communication and flexibility are key to refining these initiatives, allowing schools to create a culture that nurtures both personal and professional growth.

Wellbeing is not a box-ticking exercise but a dynamic, ongoing process that demands constant attention and reflection. As we move forward in our leadership journeys, let's ensure that the principles discussed in this chapter – clear communication, inclusivity, emotional intelligence and feedback loops – are embedded into the fabric of our schools. Doing so will ensure that the wellbeing of staff is not just an afterthought but a core component of our school's success.

Reflective Questions

1. **How well does your current leadership approach promote staff wellbeing?** Consider how often you provide opportunities for open communication, feedback, and staff development. Are there areas where you could be more proactive?
2. **What systems do you have in place to regularly evaluate the effectiveness of your wellbeing initiatives?** Reflect on how your school gathers feedback from staff and whether it leads to meaningful changes.
3. **How inclusive is your current school culture?** Are there policies in place that make everyone feel valued, or are some staff or students unintentionally left behind? How can you promote greater inclusivity?

4. **Do you encourage innovation and experimentation in your leadership?** How often do you create opportunities for middle leaders and staff to contribute to wellbeing strategies? Do they have the freedom and support to try new ideas?
5. **What small, incremental changes could you introduce to improve staff wellbeing?** Reflect on the concept of 'habit stacking' and how you might introduce manageable, positive habits into your school culture.

References and Further Reading

Adair, J. (2009). *Effective Leadership: How to Be a Successful Leader.* Pan Macmillan.

Ancelotti, C. (2016). *Quiet Leadership: Winning Hearts, Minds and Matches.* Penguin Random House.

Clear, James. (2018). *Atomic Habits: An Easy & Proven Way to Build Good Habits & Break Bad Ones.* Avery.

Dweck, Carol S. (2006). *Mindset: The New Psychology of Success.* Random House.

Ferguson, A., & Moritz, M. (2015). *Leading.* Hodder & Stoughton.

Kerr, J. (2013). *Legacy: What the All Blacks Can Teach Us About the Business of Life.* Constable.

Rossman, J. (2014). *The Amazon Way: 14 Leadership Principles Behind the World's Most Disruptive Company.* Clyde Hill Publishing.

Sharkey, J. D. (2017). *Supporting and Sustaining School Mental Health.* Routledge.

Shernoff, D., & Heary, S. (2020). *The Resilient School: A Comprehensive Guide for School Leaders.* Oxford University Press.

Sinek, S. (2009). *Start with Why: How Great Leaders Inspire Everyone to Take Action.* Portfolio/Penguin.

Souers, K., & Hall, P. (2016). *SEL in the Classroom: A Guide for School Leaders.* Solution Tree.

Weist, M. D., et al. (2021). *The Whole-School Approach to Mental Health: A Practical Guide for School Leaders.* Guilford Press.

Chapter 4
Strengths-Based Approach

In the ever-evolving landscape of education, a contentious yet transformative concept looms large – the strengths-based approach. Widely debated and occasionally dismissed as idealistic, this management and organisational strategy challenges the traditional paradigm of fixing weaknesses to propel performance. Instead, it advocates for a radical shift in perspective, one that prioritises the relentless cultivation and amplification of individual and collective strengths.

At its core, the strengths-based approach represents a bold departure from conventional wisdom. It dares to defy the status quo by shining a spotlight on the inherent brilliance and untapped potential residing within each educator and school community. Rather than dwelling on deficiencies or shortcomings, this approach champions a celebration of strengths – those unique attributes and capabilities that define and distinguish individuals and teams.

Embracing the strengths-based approach is not merely an exercise in optimism; it is a pragmatic acknowledgement of the power that lies dormant within every educator. It challenges us to reimagine our role not as fixers of flaws but as cultivators of greatness. By harnessing the inherent talents and passions of educators, this approach promises to unlock a reservoir of untapped potential, propelling both personal fulfilment and organisational success to unprecedented heights.

Amidst the controversy and scepticism that may surround the strengths-based approach, one undeniable truth emerges: people thrive when they are empowered to operate from a place of strength and authenticity. As we embark on this journey to revolutionise staff wellbeing in schools, let us embrace the discomfort of change and challenge the status quo. For it is only by daring to dream, to believe and to amplify the inherent greatness within each educator that we can truly unlock the transformative power of the strengths-based approach.

Strengths-Based vs. Deficit Model

A strengths-based approach is a way of looking at individuals or groups that focuses on their positive attributes, abilities and potential. This approach emphasises building on existing resources and capabilities to achieve desired outcomes, rather than focusing on deficits or shortcomings. It emphasises what is going well and what can be improved.

On the other hand, a deficit approach is a way of looking at individuals or groups that focuses on their shortcomings, problems or deficits. This approach tends to emphasise what is not working and what needs to be fixed. It often leads to a negative outlook and can result in a lack of motivation or self-esteem.

Deficit Model: Example

In 2022, there were five Secretaries of State; four Ministers of State for Schools; four Children's Ministers; and three Skills, Apprenticeships and Higher Education Ministers... Resulting in no coherent policy making on any issue. Little investment in post-COVID catch-up. The Schools Bill that emerged from the White Paper was rushed and, ultimately, killed by the government. We still await further news on SEND.

Teacher recruitment is at 'crisis level' (TES, Jan 23). The number of secondary entrants to initial teacher training dropped by 26 per cent last year compared to 2019. Teacher shortages in key subjects e.g. Maths. Non-specialists are frequently teaching subjects they are not qualified to teach. The cuts are hitting poorer communities and the most vulnerable. Special schools have twice the proportion of temporarily filled vacant posts. In the meantime, Sunak has announced that Maths will be studied by all 16–18-year-olds...without the funding or staff or any consideration of how to tackle the recruitment crisis.

Some school buildings are now deemed unsafe due to the legacy of underfunding on school estates.

This passage exhibits a deficit approach because it primarily focuses on highlighting problems, shortcomings and failures within the education system, without offering proactive solutions or emphasising the strengths and resources available.

Strengths-Based Approach: Example

One of the key strengths of the UK education system is its rigorous academic standards. According to a report by the Organisation for Economic Co-operation and Development (OECD), the UK ranks among the top countries in the world for reading, mathematics and science literacy.

Additionally, the UK is home to some of the world's most prestigious universities, including Oxford and Cambridge, which consistently rank among the top institutions globally.

Another strength of the UK education system is its emphasis on teacher training and professional development. According to the Department for Education, over 90 per cent of teachers in the UK hold a teaching qualification, and the majority of teachers engage in professional development activities each year.

A further strength is the provision of free education to all children in the UK, regardless of their socio-economic background.

In addition, the UK education system is known for its diversity and adaptability. There are a variety of different types of schools, including state-funded schools, independent schools and special schools for children with additional needs.

Overall, the passage takes a strengths-based approach by emphasising the positive aspects and achievements of the UK education system, thereby promoting a more optimistic and empowering narrative about education in the UK.

Strengths-Based Approach in Practice

While the strengths-based approach is transformative, it is also essential to recognise that it does not ignore areas where staff may need further support. Realistically, there are aspects of any role that can be challenging, and acknowledging these areas is crucial for providing comprehensive support. For instance, identifying where a staff member may be struggling and offering guidance can be incredibly beneficial. This approach is about balancing the celebration of strengths with the recognition of needs.

In education, this means not only drawing upon the strengths of educators but also being attuned to where they might need additional support. For example, a teacher might excel in creating engaging lesson plans but struggle with classroom management. By acknowledging this need, school leaders can provide targeted support, such as professional development opportunities or mentorship programmes, to help the teacher improve in this area.

One real-world example of this balanced approach can be seen in the leadership of Oprah Winfrey. While primarily known as a media mogul and philanthropist, Oprah has made significant contributions to education through the Oprah Winfrey Leadership Academy for Girls in South Africa. Oprah's approach to leadership at the academy emphasises the importance of nurturing the strengths of her staff while also providing the necessary support to address their challenges. Her commitment to creating a supportive and empowering environment for educators highlights the impact that a strengths-based approach can have when combined with a recognition of individual needs.

Oprah's leadership at the academy is a testament to the power of balancing strengths with support. She understands that while it is essential to celebrate and cultivate the unique talents of each staff member, it is equally important to provide guidance and resources to help them overcome obstacles. This holistic approach ensures that educators are not only empowered to excel in their areas of strength but also supported in areas where they may face difficulties. Oprah expects and demands the best from her staff because she knows that their success directly impacts the students' success. By fostering a culture of excellence and support, she ensures that the staff can perform at their highest potential, ultimately benefiting the students.

As we move forward in our leadership journeys, it is essential to ensure that the principles discussed in this chapter – clear communication, inclusivity, emotional intelligence and feedback loops – are embedded into the fabric of our schools. Doing so will ensure that the wellbeing of staff is not just an afterthought but a core component of our school's success.

What Does the Academic Literature Say?

In the realm of staff wellbeing in schools, a strengths-based approach offers a transformative perspective, emphasising the cultivation of individuals' unique abilities and talents over fixing their weaknesses. Inspired by Martin

Seligman's groundbreaking work in positive psychology, this approach encourages educators to shift their focus from remedying deficiencies to harnessing strengths. Seligman's insights, as outlined in his book *Authentic Happiness* (2002), underscore the importance of recognising and leveraging one's inherent strengths to promote wellbeing and fulfilment.

Tom Rath, in his book *StrengthsFinder 2.0* (2007), further emphasises the power of focusing on strengths. He posits that when individuals align their work with their strengths, they become more engaged, motivated and successful. This principle holds significant implications for staff wellbeing in schools, suggesting that by empowering educators to capitalise on their strengths, schools can cultivate a more positive and thriving work environment.

Carlo Ancelotti's leadership provides a compelling example of the transformative impact of a strengths-based approach. Through his coaching philosophy, Ancelotti demonstrated a commitment to nurturing the strengths of his team members rather than dwelling on their weaknesses. His approach, as illustrated in his memoir *Quiet Leadership* (2016) enabled individuals to flourish and achieve remarkable success, including becoming European Champions within a remarkably short timeframe.

Zlatan Ibrahimović's testimony further underscores the efficacy of a strengths-based approach in coaching. Reflecting on his experience under Ancelotti's guidance, Ibrahimović recalls a pivotal shift in perspective. Ancelotti's emphasis on focusing on strengths rather than conforming to traditional expectations empowered Ibrahimović to play to his strengths, leading to unprecedented success on the field (Ibrahimović, 2011).

In *The Power of Positive Leadership* (2017), Jon Gordon advocates for a strengths-based approach to leadership, particularly in the context of staff wellbeing in schools. The book highlights the transformative power of positive psychology, emphasising how a positive mindset and attitude among educators can lead to a culture of excellence and positivity. By focusing on strengths rather than weaknesses, leaders can enhance communication, collaboration and productivity within their teams. Gordon provides practical strategies such as setting clear goals, offering regular feedback and recognising and rewarding success, which help leaders identify and develop the strengths of their team members. This approach empowers educators to create an environment where staff feel valued, motivated and capable of performing at their best.

Additionally, the book stresses the importance of fostering a culture of continuous improvement. By encouraging educators to set ambitious goals and embrace new challenges, leaders can support the ongoing development of staff strengths, further enhancing the overall wellbeing and effectiveness of the school community. Although the book is primarily aimed at the business world, its principles are highly relevant to education. By implementing the strategies from *The Power of Positive Leadership*, educators can create a more positive and supportive learning environment, ultimately benefiting both students and staff.

Insights from Nike

In the realm of staff wellbeing and organisational culture within schools, *Shoe Dog: A Memoir by the Creator of Nike* (2016) by Phil Knight offers invaluable insights into building a successful and thriving community. Through the lens of Nike's early days and its evolution into a global powerhouse, Knight delves into the principles that underpinned the company's culture and success.

Central to Nike's ethos was the empowerment of employees, a concept deeply rooted in the idea of autonomy and creative freedom. Knight vividly describes how Nike fostered an environment where individuals were encouraged to take risks, think innovatively and pursue excellence in their roles. By providing employees with the autonomy and resources needed to excel, Nike cultivated a culture of empowerment and ownership, essential components of staff wellbeing and satisfaction.

Knight emphasises the value of diversity within the company's leadership team, highlighting the importance of assembling individuals with diverse strengths and abilities. By harnessing the collective talents of its team members, Nike was able to create a dynamic and cohesive leadership structure that drove the company's success. Nike's culture embraced the idea of setting stretch goals and embracing new challenges as opportunities for development. This commitment to ongoing learning and advancement not only fuelled individual growth but also contributed to the company's overall success.

Shoe Dog isn't just a memoir; it's a masterclass in crafting a culture of triumph against all odds. Its pages pulse with the relentless pursuit of excellence and the unwavering belief in the power of a unified team. As educators, we're not just reading about a sneaker empire; we're delving into the very essence of what drives success in any endeavour. From Phil Knight's journey, we learn that fostering a culture of empowerment, diversity and relentless pursuit of improvement isn't just a business strategy – it's the heartbeat of organisational greatness. It's a wake-up call to reimagine our schools as vibrant ecosystems where every member feels valued, supported and inspired to soar. Shoe Dog isn't just a memoir; it's a manifesto for building educational environments where staff wellbeing isn't just a priority – it's a non-negotiable cornerstone of excellence.

How Can We Use a Strengths-Based Approach in Schools?

Inset Days

Inset days present a valuable opportunity for educators to come together and engage in professional development that not only enhances their teaching skills but also nurtures their personal growth and wellbeing. By incorporating a strengths-based approach into these sessions, schools can create a culture of empowerment and positivity among their staff.

The day can commence with an activity where each participant reflects on and shares their own strengths. This exercise not only allows individuals to recognise and celebrate their unique abilities but also fosters a sense of appreciation and mutual respect within the team. By acknowledging the diverse strengths present among staff members, educators can cultivate a supportive and collaborative environment where everyone feels valued and empowered.

Following this introspective exercise, the focus can shift towards identifying the strengths inherent within the school as a whole. Educators can engage in discussions and activities aimed at recognising the collective talents and resources that contribute to the school's success. By highlighting the strengths of the school community, staff members can develop a deeper sense of pride and ownership in their shared mission of providing quality education and support to students.

Once individual and collective strengths have been acknowledged, the inset day can then transition into exploring ways to further develop and leverage these strengths. Workshops, presentations and collaborative activities can be organised to help educators identify strategies for incorporating their strengths into their teaching practices, fostering innovation and maximising student engagement. Additionally, discussions on personal development plans and goal-setting can empower staff members to actively pursue opportunities for growth and self-improvement in alignment with their strengths.

Throughout the day, emphasis should be placed on the positive impact of a strengths-based approach on both individual wellbeing and organisational effectiveness. By embracing and leveraging their strengths, educators can experience greater job satisfaction, resilience and fulfilment in their roles. Moreover, a strengths-based school culture promotes collaboration, innovation and continuous improvement, ultimately benefiting the entire school community.

Inset days are often squandered opportunities, used merely as a platform for senior leadership teams to push their own agendas and perpetuate deficit-focused approaches to professional development. Instead of nurturing the talents and potential of educators, these days are often hijacked by top-down directives and one-size-fits-all training sessions that fail to address the unique needs and strengths of individual staff members.

It's time to reclaim the purpose of inset days and harness their potential to empower educators through a strengths-based approach. By shifting the focus from deficits to strengths, schools can transform these days into transformative experiences that cultivate a culture of empowerment, collaborationor and innovation.

Inset days should be a time for educators to come together and celebrate their individual and collective strengths. Rather than being subjected to rigid agendas and imposed training modules, staff members should be encouraged to share their expertise, insights and experiences in a supportive and inclusive environment.

Furthermore, inset days should provide opportunities for educators to explore how they can leverage their strengths to enhance their teaching practice, foster creativity, and maximise student engagement. Workshops, peer-led discussions, and collaborative projects can empower educators to take ownership of their professional development journey and pursue areas of growth that align with their strengths and interests.

It's time to break free from the constraints of traditional professional development models and embrace a strengths-based approach that honours the diverse talents and contributions of educators. By investing in the personal and professional development of staff members and creating a culture of appreciation and empowerment, schools can unlock the full potential of their workforce and create environments where both educators and students thrive.

Team Meetings

Traditional staff meetings often fall victim to inefficiency and lack of engagement, becoming mundane gatherings where valuable time is wasted on administrative tasks and irrelevant discussions. Instead of serving as platforms for collaboration and growth, these meetings can feel like obligatory checkboxes on the calendar, draining energy and enthusiasm from educators.

It's time to reimagine team meetings as dynamic and purposeful gatherings that prioritise collaboration, innovation and professional growth. Rather than adhering to rigid agendas dictated by senior leadership, team meetings should be spaces where educators come together to share ideas, problem-solve and support one another in their quest for excellence.

By embracing a strengths-based approach to team meetings, schools can harness the collective expertise and talents of their staff members to drive meaningful change and innovation. Each meeting can be structured to allow educators to showcase their strengths and expertise, whether it's through leading discussions, sharing best practices or delivering mini CPD sessions on their areas of expertise.

Imagine the impact of dedicating just five minutes of each team meeting to a staff member delivering CPD on their area of strength. Not only does this empower educators to take ownership of their professional development, but it also fosters a culture of collaboration and mutual support within the team. Instead of being passive recipients of top-down directives, educators become active participants in their own growth and development journey.

Team meetings should be more than just routine gatherings – they should be dynamic platforms for collaboration and growth. It's time to break away from the limitations of traditional staff meetings and embrace a bold new approach that empowers and inspires. By shifting the focus from top-down directives to bottom-up collaboration and expertise sharing, schools can unlock the full potential of their staff and foster a culture of innovation and excellence. Let's challenge the status quo and transform team meetings into powerful catalysts for positive change and professional advancement.

Quality Assurance

In the realm of quality assurance, there's often a tendency to prioritise identifying areas of improvement, sometimes overlooking the strengths and successes already present within our school community. However, what if we approached quality assurance from a different angle, one that begins by highlighting what's already working well?

Imagine conducting lesson observations and book looks that focus exclusively on identifying and celebrating the positives. By adopting this strengths-based approach, we can shine a light on the effective teaching strategies, student engagement techniques and exemplary work found within our classrooms and exercise books. Rather than searching for flaws or shortcomings, these observations and book looks become opportunities to recognise and amplify the strengths that contribute to a vibrant and successful learning environment.

Moreover, incorporating learning walks into our quality assurance processes allows us to extend this positive mindset beyond individual lessons and assignments. As we roam the corridors, engaging with students and staff alike, we can actively seek out instances of innovation, collaboration and effective practice. From interactive displays showcasing student achievements to teachers implementing creative instructional methods, there's much to be celebrated and learned from throughout our school community.

By focusing on strengths during quality assurance activities, we not only foster a culture of positivity and appreciation but also empower our educators to build upon their successes. Through targeted feedback and professional development opportunities tailored to amplify existing strengths, we can further enhance teaching and learning outcomes. Ultimately, this approach cultivates a school environment where positivity, growth and continuous improvement flourish.

Appraisal

In the realm of staff appraisal, traditional approaches often centre around identifying areas for improvement or addressing perceived weaknesses. However, what if we reframed the entire appraisal cycle to prioritise recognising and leveraging strengths?

Imagine an appraisal process that begins by celebrating the achievements, accomplishments and strengths of each staff member. Instead of dwelling on shortcomings, this strengths-based approach highlights the unique talents, skills and contributions that individuals bring to our school community. By shifting the focus to what's already working well, we create a foundation of positivity and empowerment from which to build upon.

As part of this strengths-focused appraisal cycle, we could introduce a system of partnering staff members based on complementary strengths. By pairing individuals with similar strengths or complementary skill sets, we create opportunities for collaboration, mentorship and mutual growth. These partnerships serve as catalysts for personal and professional development, as individuals learn from one another and support each other's growth journeys.

These strength-based partnerships can extend beyond the formal appraisal process, becoming integral components of our school culture. Through ongoing collaboration and feedback exchanges, staff members can continue to identify ways to leverage their strengths, address challenges and maximise their potential. Whether through peer coaching, collaborative projects or shared learning experiences, these partnerships foster a culture of continuous improvement and collective success.

By embedding a strengths-based approach into the fabric of our staff appraisal cycle, we not only recognise and honour the diverse talents and contributions of our team but also create a culture of support, growth, and excellence. Through intentional focus on strengths, we empower each staff member to thrive personally and professionally, driving positive outcomes for both individuals and the school community as a whole.

PERMAH – What Is It?

The PERMAH approach is an extension of the well-known PERMA model of wellbeing proposed by positive psychology pioneer Martin Seligman. The original PERMA model identifies five core elements of wellbeing: Positive emotions, Engagement, Relationships, Meaning and Accomplishment. Building upon this framework, the PERMAH model adds two additional components: Health and Habits.

The PERMAH model was developed by Sue Langley and was first introduced in her book *Positive Relationships at Work: How to Create Productive, Engaging, and Collaborative Workplaces* (2019). Langley's model emphasises the importance of health and habits in contributing to overall wellbeing, recognising that physical health and positive habits play significant roles in shaping individuals' experiences of happiness and fulfilment.

The addition of Health to the PERMA model acknowledges the essential role that physical health plays in overall wellbeing. Research has consistently shown a strong connection between physical health and psychological wellbeing, with factors such as exercise, nutrition, sleep and stress management playing critical roles in promoting optimal functioning and life satisfaction (Boehm & Kubsansky, 2012; Diener et al., 2017).

Similarly, the inclusion of Habits in the PERMAH model highlights the impact of daily routines and behaviours on individuals' wellbeing outcomes. Positive habits, such as practising gratitude, mindfulness and kindness, have been linked to increased levels of happiness and resilience, while negative habits, such as rumination and avoidance, can undermine mental health and wellbeing (Lyubomirsky et al., 2005; Duckworth et al., 2005).

By incorporating Health and Habits into the PERMA framework, the PERMAH model provides a holistic and comprehensive approach to understanding and promoting wellbeing. By addressing all seven elements – Positive emotions, Engagement, Relationships, Meaning, Accomplishment, Health and Habits – individuals can cultivate a more balanced and fulfilling life, characterised by greater happiness, resilience and overall satisfaction.

How Does PERMAH Link to Schools?

The PERMAH model offers a comprehensive framework for promoting staff wellbeing in schools. Each component of PERMAH – Positive emotions, Engagement, Relationships, Meaning, Accomplishment and Health and Habits – can be tailored to support the wellbeing of staff members, thereby creating a positive and supportive work environment.

Positive Emotions

Fostering positive emotions among educators is crucial for promoting their overall wellbeing and creating a supportive work environment. Staff wellbeing initiatives can incorporate various strategies to cultivate positive emotions and enhance morale.

- You could introduce mindfulness practices into the daily routine of educators. Mindfulness exercises, such as guided meditation sessions or mindful breathing exercises, can help staff members reduce stress, increase self-awareness and cultivate a sense of calm and balance. By providing opportunities for educators to engage in mindfulness practices, schools can support their mental and emotional wellbeing.

- Gratitude exercises are another powerful tool for fostering positive emotions among educators. Encouraging staff members to reflect on and express gratitude for the things they appreciate in their professional lives can enhance their overall sense of happiness and satisfaction. Schools can implement gratitude journals, gratitude circles or regular gratitude rituals to encourage staff members to focus on the positive aspects of their work and relationships.
- Appreciation programmes can play a significant role in promoting positive emotions among educators. Recognising and celebrating achievements, both big and small, can boost morale and motivation. Schools can establish formal recognition programmes, such as 'Staff Member of the Month' awards or 'Kudos Boards' where colleagues can publicly acknowledge each other's accomplishments. Furthermore, leaders can express appreciation through personalised notes, verbal praise during staff meetings or small tokens of appreciation to show gratitude for their hard work and dedication.

Engagement

Encouraging staff members to find activities that resonate with their passions and interests is crucial for fostering engagement and enhancing their overall wellbeing. This can involve offering a variety of opportunities for professional development, creativity and autonomy within the school community.

- Professional development programmes tailored to individual interests and career goals can empower educators to pursue continuous learning and growth. This could include workshops, seminars, conferences or online courses covering a wide range of topics relevant to their teaching practice and personal development. By investing in their professional growth, educators feel valued and supported, leading to increased job satisfaction and commitment to their roles.
- Opportunities for creativity allow staff members to express themselves and explore innovative approaches to teaching and learning. This could involve encouraging educators to incorporate new technologies, teaching methods or interdisciplinary approaches into their lesson plans. Creating a culture that celebrates experimentation and risk-taking fosters a sense

of excitement and ownership among staff members, driving engagement and creativity.
- Autonomy plays a crucial role in empowering educators to take ownership of their work and make meaningful contributions to the school community. Allowing teachers the flexibility to design their own curriculum, choose instructional materials and implement teaching strategies that align with their strengths and interests fosters a sense of autonomy and responsibility. When educators have a sense of control over their work environment, they are more likely to feel invested in their roles and motivated to excel.

Relationships

Building positive relationships among staff members and between staff and leadership is a cornerstone of promoting staff wellbeing in schools.

- The implementation of mentorship programmes can support and develop positive relationships. These programmes pair experienced educators with newer staff members, providing them with guidance, support and professional development opportunities. Mentors can offer valuable insights, share best practices and help new staff navigate the challenges of their roles, ultimately fostering a sense of belonging and support within the school community.
- Collaborative projects also play a crucial role in strengthening bonds among staff members. By encouraging educators to work together on interdisciplinary projects, curriculum development or school-wide initiatives, schools can promote collaboration, creativity and shared ownership of the school's mission and goals. Collaborative projects provide opportunities for staff members to leverage their diverse skills and expertise, fostering a sense of teamwork and camaraderie.
- Team-building activities further contribute to the cultivation of positive relationships within the school community. These activities can range from informal social gatherings to structured team-building exercises designed to improve communication, trust and cooperation among staff members. By engaging in team-building activities, educators can develop stronger connections with their colleagues, break down barriers and build a sense of community and solidarity.

- Open communication and feedback are essential for nurturing positive relationships within the school community. Regular staff meetings, forums and feedback sessions provide avenues for staff members to voice their ideas, concerns and suggestions, fostering a culture of transparency, trust and collaboration. When staff members feel heard, valued and respected, they are more likely to develop meaningful connections with their colleagues and feel a sense of belonging within the school community.

Meaning

Helping staff members find meaning and purpose in their roles is crucial for their overall satisfaction and wellbeing.

- One way to achieve this is by providing opportunities for professional growth and development. This can include offering workshops, training sessions and conferences that allow staff members to enhance their skills, learn new teaching strategies and stay updated on the latest educational trends. Additionally, providing access to resources such as online courses, certifications and mentoring programmes can empower educators to continuously improve and advance in their careers.
- Leadership development is another important aspect of fostering meaning and purpose among staff members. Schools can offer leadership training programmes, coaching sessions and mentorship opportunities to help educators develop their leadership skills and take on leadership roles within the school community. By nurturing leadership potential and providing avenues for growth, schools can inspire staff members to make meaningful contributions and take ownership of their professional development.
- Creating opportunities for staff members to make meaningful contributions to the school community is also key to enhancing job satisfaction and fulfilment. This can involve involving staff in decision-making processes, encouraging them to share their ideas and expertise, and giving them a voice in shaping school policies and initiatives. Additionally, recognising and celebrating the contributions of staff members through awards, acknowledgements and appreciation events can reinforce their sense of purpose and value within the school community.

Accomplishment

Accomplishment is a vital aspect of staff wellbeing in schools, as it involves recognising and celebrating the achievements of educators, which can significantly boost morale and motivation.

- Establishing a culture of recognition and appreciation within the school community is key to this. This can involve regular acknowledgement of individual and team achievements through public announcements, awards ceremonies or appreciation events.
- Setting clear goals and expectations for educators is essential for fostering a sense of accomplishment. By defining specific objectives and milestones, educators have a clear roadmap for success and can track their progress towards achieving their goals. Additionally, providing regular feedback on performance allows educators to understand their strengths and areas for improvement, enabling them to make meaningful progress in their roles.
- Offering support for professional growth and career advancement is crucial for empowering educators to thrive in their roles. This can include opportunities for ongoing training, professional development workshops and access to resources that help educators enhance their skills and expertise. By investing in the growth and development of staff members, schools demonstrate their commitment to supporting the success and wellbeing of their educators.

Health and Fitness

Prioritising the physical and mental health of staff members encompasses a multifaceted approach aimed at enhancing their overall wellbeing and resilience. Schools can implement various initiatives and strategies to support educators in maintaining their health and vitality.

- Establishing comprehensive wellness programmes that address various aspects of health, including physical, emotional and social wellbeing, is crucial. These programmes can include fitness classes, mindfulness sessions, nutrition workshops, stress management seminars and relaxation techniques. By offering a diverse range of activities, educators can find

options that resonate with their preferences and needs, fostering a culture of holistic wellness within the school community.
- Collaborating with local healthcare providers, fitness professionals and mental health experts can enrich wellness initiatives. These partnerships enable schools to access specialised expertise and resources, ensuring that wellness programmes are evidence-based and effectively tailored to the unique needs of educators. By engaging external partners, schools can broaden their scope and reach, providing staff members with comprehensive support for their health and wellbeing.
- Providing access to mental health resources and support services is paramount. Educators face various stressors and challenges in their roles, and having access to counselling, therapy and employee assistance programmes (EAPs) can be invaluable. By normalising conversations about mental health and destigmatising help-seeking behaviours, schools create a supportive environment where staff members feel empowered to prioritise their emotional wellbeing. This proactive approach not only supports individual educators but also fosters a culture of empathy and understanding within the school community.

By integrating the principles of PERMAH into staff wellbeing initiatives, schools can create a positive and supportive work environment that fosters the wellbeing and success of all staff members.

Conclusion

In this chapter, we've explored the transformative potential of strengths-based approaches and the PERMAH model in enhancing staff wellbeing within schools. By focusing on the unique strengths of individuals and fostering positive habits, we shift the narrative away from deficits and toward a more empowering framework for development. This not only supports the emotional and mental health of staff but also cultivates a culture where excellence and wellbeing go hand in hand.

At the heart of these approaches lies the recognition that staff wellbeing isn't a one-size-fits-all process. Schools must foster an environment where educators feel valued for their individual talents, where positive relationships and a sense of meaning in their roles are prioritised. By embracing PERMAH's core elements – Positive emotions, Engagement, Relationships,

Meaning, Accomplishment, and Health –we can create a school culture that not only drives professional satisfaction but also encourages personal fulfilment and resilience.

Quality assurance processes are essential in this journey, ensuring that policies and wellbeing initiatives remain effective and relevant. Through regular reflection, feedback and adjustments, schools can continue to support staff in a meaningful way, enabling them to thrive both professionally and personally.

As you reflect on the ideas presented in this chapter, consider how your own leadership and the systems in place at your school can better align with a strengths-based approach. Remember, the key to success lies not in fixing weaknesses but in amplifying the strengths that already exist within your team.

Reflective Questions

1. **How do you currently identify and celebrate the strengths of your staff?** Reflect on whether your school has mechanisms in place to recognise individual talents and how these can be further nurtured.
2. **What opportunities exist for staff to engage with their personal passions and strengths in the workplace?** Are there areas where you could introduce more autonomy, creativity or professional development opportunities aligned with their interests?
3. **How do you foster positive relationships and a sense of belonging among staff?** Consider whether your team has regular opportunities for collaboration, feedback and support.
4. **What structures are in place to promote physical and mental wellbeing in your school?** Reflect on whether your school offers resources or programmes that encourage staff to prioritise their health and work–life balance.
5. **How do you measure the success of your wellbeing initiatives?** Do you have quality assurance mechanisms in place to evaluate and refine these programmes regularly based on feedback?

References and Further Reading

Ancelotti, C. (2016). *Quiet Leadership: Winning Hearts, Minds and Matches*. Penguin Random House.

Boehm, J. K., & Kubzansky, L. D. (2012). 'The heart's content: The association between positive psychological well-being and cardiovascular health.' *Psychological Bulletin, 138*(4), 655–691. https://doi.org/10.1037/a0027448

Diener, E., Pressman, S. D., Hunter, J., & Delgadillo-Chase, D. (2017). 'If, why, and when subjective well-being influences health, and future needed research.' *Applied Psychology: Health and Well-Being, 9*(2), 133–167. https://doi.org/10.1111/aphw.12090

Duckworth, A. L., Peterson, C., Matthews, M. D., & Kelly, D. R. (2007). 'Grit: Perseverance and passion for long-term goals.' *Journal of Personality and Social Psychology, 92*(6), 1087–1101. https://doi.org/10.1037/0022-3514.92.6.1087

Gordon, J. (2017). *The Power of Positive Leadership: How and Why Positive Leaders Transform Teams and Organizations and Change the World*. John Wiley & Sons.

Ibrahimović, Zlatan. (2011). *I Am Zlatan Ibrahimović*. Penguin Books.

Knight, P. (2016). *Shoe Dog: A Memoir by the Creator of Nike*. Scribner.

Langley, S. (2019). *Positive Relationships at Work: How to Create Productive, Engaging, and Collaborative Workplaces*. John Wiley & Sons.

Lyubomirsky, S., Sheldon, K. M., & Schkade, D. (2005). 'Pursuing happiness: The architecture of sustainable change.' *Review of General Psychology, 9*(2), 111–131. https://doi.org/10.1037/1089-2680.9.2.111

Rath, T. (2007). *StrengthsFinder 2.0*. Gallup Press.

Seligman, M. E. P. (2002). *Authentic Happiness: Using the New Positive Psychology to Realize Your Potential for Lasting Fulfilment*. Free Press.

Seligman, M. E. P. (2011). *Flourish: A Visionary New Understanding of Happiness and Well-Being*. Free Press.

Chapter 5
Communication

In the realm of staff wellbeing, communication stands as the cornerstone upon which effective collaboration, trust and support are built. Just as Patrick Lencioni's seminal work, *The Five Dysfunctions of a Team: A Leadership Fable*, illuminates the critical role of communication in fostering cohesive teamwork, so too does it underscore its profound significance in nurturing the mental and emotional health of staff.

In Lencioni's narrative, the absence of open, honest communication serves as a catalyst for dysfunction within teams, leading to fractured relationships, diminished productivity and, ultimately, organisational failure. Equally, within the context of staff wellbeing, ineffective communication can sow seeds of mistrust, isolation and burnout among staff, perpetuating a cycle of disengagement and dissatisfaction.

Nonetheless, just as Lencioni's fable offers a beacon of hope through the transformational power of authentic communication, so too does it inspire us to recognise the immense potential for positive change within our educational communities. By adopting a culture of transparent dialogue, active listening and genuine empathy, staff can cultivate environments where voices are heard, ideas are valued and support is readily available.

Effective communication lies at the heart of creating a nurturing environment for staff wellbeing. By establishing open and transparent channels of communication, schools can facilitate collaboration, address concerns and cultivate a sense of belonging among staff members.

Communication serves as a vital tool for sharing resources, strategies and best practices among staff. When teachers have access to clear and reliable channels for sharing ideas and resources, they can draw upon each other's expertise and experience to enhance their practice. Whether it's through staff meetings, digital platforms or informal conversations, fostering a culture of communication enables staff to support one another in their professional growth and development.

Moreover, open communication channels play a crucial role in addressing concerns and challenges that arise within the school community. When staff members feel comfortable expressing their opinions, raising issues and seeking support, it creates a culture of trust and transparency. By actively listening to the needs and perspectives of staff members, school leadership can identify areas for improvement and take proactive steps to address them, fostering a supportive and inclusive environment for all.

Additionally, effective communication contributes to building a sense of community and belonging among staff members. When educators feel that their voices are heard and valued, it enhances their sense of agency and ownership within the school community. By creating opportunities for collaboration, feedback and dialogue, schools can strengthen relationships and foster a shared commitment to the wellbeing and success of all staff members.

In this chapter, we explore the importance of effective communication in supporting staff wellbeing within educational settings. Drawing upon principles of openness, transparency and collaboration, we examine strategies for establishing communication channels that empower educators, promote collaboration and cultivate a culture of support and belonging within schools. Through real-world examples and practical insights, we demonstrate how effective communication can serve as a cornerstone for nurturing staff wellbeing and creating thriving school communities.

Staff Meetings

Regular staff meetings play a pivotal role in fostering staff wellbeing within educational institutions. These gatherings serve as vital platforms where teachers can come together to openly discuss concerns, share innovative ideas and provide constructive feedback. By prioritising inclusivity and encouraging active participation from all staff members, leaders can cultivate a culture of collaboration, trust and mutual support.

Effective leaders recognise the importance of structuring staff meetings in a way that promotes engagement and facilitates meaningful dialogue. For instance, leaders may adopt strategies such as agenda-setting to ensure that key topics are addressed and sufficient time is allocated for discussion. Additionally, they may leverage technology platforms or interactive tools to encourage participation and gather feedback from attendees in real time.

An exemplary example of effective meeting leadership comes from the business world, specifically from Alan Mulally, the former CEO of Ford Motor Company. Mulally was renowned for his exceptional ability to conduct meetings that were focused, collaborative and results-driven. He implemented a weekly meeting called the 'Business Plan Review' (BPR), where leaders from different departments would come together to review progress, share updates and identify areas for improvement.

During these meetings, Mulally fostered an environment of transparency and accountability by encouraging open communication and constructive feedback. He emphasised the importance of addressing challenges head-on and working collaboratively to find solutions. By creating a culture of trust and empowerment, Mulally ensured that everyone felt valued and invested in the company's success.

Moreover, effective leaders like Mulally recognise the importance of follow-up and accountability in ensuring that issues discussed during staff meetings are addressed in a timely manner. They take proactive steps to implement action plans, monitor progress and provide feedback to staff members, demonstrating their commitment to continuous improvement and employee satisfaction.

Jeff Bezos, the founder and former CEO of Amazon, is renowned for his innovative approach to leadership and management. One notable practice he implemented in Amazon's corporate culture is the inclusion of dedicated reading time during meetings. This unique strategy reflects Bezos's commitment to fostering a culture of learning, critical thinking and intellectual curiosity within the company.

During meetings at Amazon, Bezos often starts by allocating time for all participants to read through a detailed memo or proposal. These documents, known as 'narratives', are meticulously crafted by team members to outline key ideas, proposals or strategic initiatives. By requiring everyone to read the memo before discussions commence, Bezos ensures that all participants are on the same page and have a deep understanding of the topic at hand.

The practice of incorporating reading time into meetings serves several purposes. First, it encourages thorough preparation and active engagement among attendees, as they are required to familiarise themselves with the content beforehand. This helps streamline discussions and allows for more meaningful exchanges of ideas and insights during the meeting.

Moreover, Bezos believes that written narratives promote clarity, precision and depth of thought in communication. Rather than relying solely on oral presentations or PowerPoint slides, the use of written documents encourages team members to articulate their ideas in a coherent and compelling manner. This approach fosters a culture of rigorous analysis and thoughtful decision-making within the organisation.

Bezos's emphasis on reading time also reflects his belief in the power of long-form thinking and the value of deep reading. In a fast-paced and information-saturated world, taking the time to immerse oneself in detailed written content can lead to deeper understanding, broader perspectives and more informed decision-making. By prioritising reading as an essential part of the meeting process, Bezos encourages intellectual curiosity and continuous learning among Amazon's leadership team.

Principles of an Effective Meeting

Effective staff meetings are essential for fostering collaboration, communication and morale among team members. Incorporating certain principles can help make these meetings more engaging, productive and enjoyable for everyone involved.

First and foremost, it's crucial to keep the meeting concise and adhere to the scheduled time. Respect for everyone's time is paramount, so having a clear agenda and sticking to it ensures that discussions remain focused and efficient. Additionally, starting and ending the meeting on time demonstrates professionalism and reinforces the importance of punctuality.

Injecting humour and levity into the meeting can help create a positive and inclusive atmosphere. A light-hearted joke or amusing anecdote can break the ice, relieve tension and encourage team members to engage more freely. However, it's important to strike a balance and ensure that humour is appropriate and respectful to all participants. Including fun quizzes or interactive activities can add an element of excitement and enjoyment to staff meetings. Incorporating games or trivia questions can energise participants, stimulate cognitive engagement and promote team bonding. These activities can also serve as valuable learning opportunities and help reinforce key concepts or objectives discussed during the meeting.

Avoiding lectures and fostering interactive discussions is another key principle of effective staff meetings. Instead of monologues or one-way presentations, encourage dialogue, brainstorming and idea-sharing among team members. This allows everyone to contribute their insights, experiences and perspectives, leading to richer discussions and better outcomes.

Taking a strengths-based approach during staff meetings can also enhance engagement and motivation among team members. Acknowledge and celebrate individual strengths, accomplishments and contributions during the meeting to boost morale and foster a sense of appreciation and recognition. This can be done through shout-outs, awards or spotlighting specific achievements.

Encouraging collaboration and teamwork is essential for maximising the collective potential of the group. Provide opportunities for team members to collaborate on projects, share resources and support each other's initiatives. By fostering a collaborative environment, staff meetings become more dynamic and productive, leading to innovative solutions and stronger team cohesion.

Finally, recognising staff achievements and milestones is essential for boosting morale and motivation. Take time during the meeting to celebrate individual and team accomplishments, whether it's reaching goals, completing projects or demonstrating exceptional performance. Recognising and applauding staff achievements not only boosts morale but also reinforces a culture of appreciation and support within the team.

Incorporating these principles into staff meetings can help create a positive, engaging and productive environment where team members feel valued, motivated and inspired to contribute their best.

Death by Meetings

'Death by meetings' is a common phrase heard in workplaces, including schools, where staff members often find themselves overwhelmed by lengthy and unproductive meetings. The issue with excessive meetings goes beyond time wasted; it can also have a significant impact on staff wellbeing.

Constantly attending meetings that could have been emails can lead to feelings of frustration, stress and burnout among educators and administrators. These meetings not only consume valuable time but also disrupt workflow and hinder productivity. As a result, staff members may find themselves struggling to manage their workload effectively, leading to increased levels of stress and exhaustion.

Furthermore, the repetitive nature of unnecessary meetings can contribute to feelings of disengagement and disillusionment among staff. When educators are forced to sit through meetings that do not directly contribute to their work or professional development, they may become demotivated and disenchanted with their roles.

To address this issue and prioritise staff wellbeing, schools must adopt a more mindful approach to scheduling meetings. Rather than defaulting to regular meetings as the standard mode of communication, administrators should carefully consider whether a meeting is truly necessary or if the same objectives can be achieved through alternative means, such as emails, memos or collaborative online platforms.

Listen More, Talk Less

Listening more and talking less is a fundamental principle that can profoundly impact staff wellbeing within educational institutions. Just as educators engage in dialogue with their students to foster understanding and collaboration, so too should leaders prioritise active listening in their interactions with staff members. Real-life leaders who embody this principle create environments where voices are valued, concerns are heard and solutions are collaboratively developed.

One such leader renowned for his emphasis on listening is Satya Nadella, the CEO of Microsoft. Nadella's leadership style is characterised by his commitment to empathy and understanding, traits that enable him to connect with employees on a personal level. By actively listening to their ideas, concerns and feedback, Nadella fosters a culture of openness and inclusivity within the organisation, contributing to enhanced employee morale and wellbeing.

Moreover, Nadella believes that effective communication, particularly during times of uncertainty, is crucial for maintaining clarity and stability within an organisation. His approach to communication emphasises conciseness and simplicity, ensuring that messages are clear, concise and easily understandable. For example, when announcing significant changes such as job reductions, Nadella's communication to employees is characterised by its brevity and clarity, with a focus on delivering key messages succinctly and transparently.

In Nadella's recent company-wide email announcing the elimination of 10,000 jobs, he demonstrated the power of clear communication by adhering to the rule of three – a well-established principle in neuroscience literature that suggests people find it easier to absorb and recall information presented in threes. By highlighting three priorities and articulating them in a straightforward manner, Nadella ensured that his message was easily comprehensible and memorable for employees.

Furthermore, Nadella's communication style exemplifies the importance of treating employees with dignity and respect, even in challenging circumstances. By emphasising transparency and providing details about severance packages and benefits for affected workers, Nadella demonstrates his commitment to supporting employees through difficult transitions.

Similarly, Indra Nooyi, the former CEO of PepsiCo, exemplifies the importance of listening in leadership. Nooyi's leadership philosophy emphasises the value of diverse perspectives and the power of listening to drive innovation and success. By creating opportunities for dialogue and feedback across all levels of the organisation, Nooyi ensures that employees feel heard, respected and valued, thereby promoting a positive and supportive work environment.

Nooyi exemplified the 'listen more, talk less' approach in the post-pandemic discussions about remote working by urging leaders to prioritise understanding the varied needs and experiences of employees. Rather than imposing top-down directives, she emphasised the importance of engaging in meaningful dialogue with staff and actively seeking their input on potential changes to working arrangements. By encouraging experimentation and collaboration among companies, Nooyi demonstrated a commitment to finding innovative solutions tailored to the unique circumstances of each organisation and its workforce. In doing so, she underscored the value of communication grounded in empathy, transparency and inclusivity, setting a compelling example for leaders navigating the complexities of the new work landscape.

In the context of staff meetings, adopting a 'listen more, talk less' approach can transform the dynamics and effectiveness of these gatherings. Instead of monologue-style presentations that leave little room for input, leaders can create space for meaningful dialogue and exchange of ideas. For example, utilising briefing bulletins to disseminate information can streamline meetings, allowing more time for discussion and feedback.

Feedback Mechanisms

Establishing robust feedback mechanisms is essential for promoting staff well-being in schools. Too often, teachers and associate staff feel hesitant to voice their concerns or suggestions openly, fearing potential reprisal or judgement. To address this issue, schools must implement anonymous feedback channels, such as suggestion boxes or online surveys, that provide teachers with a safe space to express their thoughts and feelings candidly. By ensuring anonymity, educators can communicate their needs and experiences without fear of repercussions, fostering a culture of trust and transparency within the school community.

It is, however, easy for me to write this and far harder for this to be implemented. Establishing robust feedback mechanisms in schools can be challenging for some senior leadership teams (SLT) for various reasons. One primary challenge is the fear of criticism or negative feedback from staff members. SLT members may worry that implementing anonymous feedback channels could lead to a flood of complaints or grievances, which they may perceive as a reflection of their leadership or management style. This fear of reprisal or judgement may deter SLT members from embracing transparency and openness in communication with staff. One way round this is by setting out some core principles with staff first. This may include not allowing staff to name individual members of staff (therefore making it less personal). Equally, it may be that for every negative comment, a positive suggestion is made.

Additionally, some SLT members may lack the necessary skills or experience to effectively manage feedback processes. Constructive feedback requires active listening, empathy and the ability to address concerns in a supportive and non-defensive manner. However, SLT members who are unfamiliar with these skills may struggle to navigate difficult conversations or respond appropriately to staff feedback, leading to further disengagement or frustration among educators. It is important therefore that one member of SLT gatekeeps the feedback. They can then sift through, pick out key areas of development while also shielding other members of SLT as appropriate. Feedback is great to hear, but when it is heard is as important as the feedback itself. Never conduct staff voice before a holiday; people are tired, and emotions run high. Equally, do it small but often, and design some feedback to catch the positives.

Finally, there may be institutional barriers or cultural norms within the school that inhibit the adoption of robust feedback mechanisms. In some cases, there may be a hierarchical structure or a top-down approach to decision-making, where staff members feel powerless or marginalised in expressing their opinions. Changing these entrenched dynamics requires a concerted effort to shift the organisational culture towards one that values transparency, collaboration and mutual respect. The best way to do this is via a 'You Said, We Did' approach. Put this on as staff come into a meeting, on an email/Teams bulletin or up in the staff room. Show that you have listened, and you have acted.

It is imperative to make staff voice a central component of school governance and decision-making processes. Staff members should be encouraged to voice their opinions frequently, openly and without reservation. This requires creating structured opportunities for staff to provide feedback and participate in dialogue about school policies, initiatives and practices. Schools should establish regular staff meetings, focus groups or forums dedicated to discussing staff concerns and soliciting input on matters affecting their wellbeing. Knowing what to ask what group and when is a skill. Some things need to collect all-staff feedback. Others need some small group feedback. Semi-structured interviews are good for this, as they allow for a focus to be established but also ensure the conversation can flow. In short, feedback needs to be well planned. Just putting out a Microsoft Form and hoping will produce sporadic results and feedback that is difficult to act on.

To aid this and avoid ad-hoc feedback mechanisms, schools should develop a comprehensive three-year plan specifically focused on staff wellbeing. This plan should outline strategic objectives, initiatives and resources dedicated to supporting the mental, emotional and physical health of teachers and staff members. Importantly, the plan should be punctuated regularly by staff voice, with scheduled check-ins and reviews to assess progress, gather feedback and make necessary adjustments.

By prioritising staff voice in the development and implementation of wellbeing initiatives, schools can ensure that the needs and perspectives of educators are central to decision-making processes. This proactive approach not only fosters a sense of ownership and investment among staff members but also facilitates the identification of challenges and opportunities for improvement. Ultimately, schools that prioritise feedback mechanisms and staff voice are better equipped to create environments where educators feel valued, supported and empowered to thrive personally and professionally.

Calendar

There are few structural elements in staff wellbeing planning as important as the school calendar. Get a bad one and it sets the tone for the rest of the year. The school calendar isn't just a schedule of events; it's a reflection of how much an institution values its staff. Yet, all too often, calendars are constructed with little consideration for the wellbeing of those who must adhere to them day in and day out. Take, for instance, the placement of parents' evenings. These crucial events, where teachers engage with parents to discuss their children's progress, are typically scheduled at the end of a long day or week, leaving staff exhausted and drained. Why not prioritise the mental and physical health of staff by placing parents' evenings on a day that doesn't add undue strain to their already demanding schedules? Better yet, as discussed above, why not ask them?

Consider the following:

- The timing of open evenings can significantly impact staff wellbeing. Hosting these events during the week, especially without considering the workload that follows, can lead to burnout among teachers who are expected to deliver exceptional performance both during and after the event.
- Instead of perpetuating this cycle of stress, schools should strategically plan open evenings with the wellbeing of their staff in mind.
- Consider scheduling an inset day following the event, allowing teachers the time they need to recuperate and recharge after putting forth their best efforts to showcase the school to prospective students and parents.

Middle leaders, comprising department heads, year leads and other key figures, serve as the bridge between senior leadership and front-line staff. Their unique position affords them intimate knowledge of both the strategic objectives of the school and the day-to-day realities faced by teachers in their respective departments. However, despite their crucial role, middle leaders are frequently left out of the decision-making process when it comes to shaping the school calendar.

Involving middle leaders in the review process of the school calendar can yield numerous benefits.

- Middle leaders bring a wealth of first-hand experience and insights into the operational needs and challenges within their departments. They understand the nuances of teaching timetables, the ebbs and flows of student engagement, and the impact of various events on staff workload. By harnessing their expertise, schools can ensure that the calendar aligns with the realities of classroom teaching and supports rather than hinders the efforts of educators.
- Middle leaders can offer a unique perspective on the strategic goals and priorities of the school. They can provide input on how certain events or scheduling decisions may impact the achievement of these objectives. For example, if the school aims to improve student attainment in a particular subject, middle leaders can advise on the most effective timing for assessment periods or intervention sessions to maximise student outcomes. There is nothing worse than assessment periods and data collections not aligning, meaning that the valuable data collected becomes out of date and less impactful.
- Additionally, involving middle leaders in the calendar review process fosters a sense of ownership and buy-in among staff. When staff feel that their voices are heard and their insights valued, they are more likely to be invested in the success of the calendar and committed to its implementation. This sense of empowerment can lead to greater morale, collaboration and overall staff wellbeing.

To effectively involve middle leaders in the review process, schools can implement various strategies.

- These may include holding regular meetings or workshops where middle leaders can discuss their departmental needs and provide feedback on the current calendar. This can be done virtually or by simply having a Word document where staff can add comments throughout the year. This is important, as staff will quickly forget if it isn't captured in the moment.
- Schools can also establish dedicated working groups or committees tasked with reviewing and refining the calendar, with representation from middle leaders across different departments.

It's important to recognise that a poorly designed calendar isn't just inconvenient; it directly impacts staff morale, motivation and overall wellbeing. Schools must prioritise creating calendars that support, rather than hinder, the health and happiness of their educators. It's time for a paradigm shift – one where the wellbeing of staff takes precedence over outdated scheduling practices.

Transparent Decision-Making

Transparent decision-making is a cornerstone of effective leadership in schools, crucial for promoting staff wellbeing and nurturing a culture of trust and collaboration. An exemplary figure in sports leadership known for transparent decision-making is Jürgen Klopp, the former manager of Liverpool Football Club. Klopp's leadership style emphasises openness, honesty and inclusivity, setting a remarkable example of transparent leadership in the world of sports.

Throughout his tenure at Liverpool, Klopp demonstrated a commitment to transparency in various aspects of team management and decision-making processes. One notable example is Klopp's communication with players regarding team selection and tactics. He maintained an open dialogue with the squad, explaining the rationale behind his decisions and soliciting input from players. This transparency fostered trust and mutual respect between Klopp and his players, empowering them to understand their roles within the team and contribute effectively to its success.

Additionally, Klopp was renowned for his candid and straightforward communication with fans and the media. Whether celebrating victories or addressing setbacks, Klopp provided honest assessments and insights into the team's performance, never shying away from discussing challenges or areas for improvement. This transparency cultivated a sense of unity and shared purpose among supporters, who appreciated Klopp's genuine and authentic approach to leadership.

Another example of Jürgen Klopp's transparent decision-making occurred in 2019 during Liverpool's Champions League campaign. Klopp faced a crucial decision regarding team selection for the final match against Tottenham Hotspur. One of Liverpool's star players, Roberto Firmino, had been struggling with injury concerns leading up to the match. Rather than keeping Firmino's status secret or making a last-minute decision without explanation, Klopp openly communicated with the media and fans about the situation. He provided updates on Firmino's condition, acknowledging the uncertainty surrounding the player's availability for the final. Some criticised him for this.

They said it provided his opponents with a tactical edge. However, Klopp recognised it was more important to take the pressure off Firmino and create an underdog culture with the fans.

Moreover, Klopp's transparent leadership extended beyond the football pitch to include engagement with club stakeholders, including owners, executives and staff. By involving all stakeholders in decision-making processes and maintaining open lines of communication, Klopp ensured that everyone was aligned with the club's goals and values, fostering a cohesive and harmonious organisational culture.

As with the school calendar, you can't leave information-sharing to chance. One of the biggest detriments to a school culture is leaks of information. It erodes trust, not only with staff but also with SLT. When a decision is made, a question which must always be asked is when, where, who, what and why are we sharing this information. Strategic sharing of information involves the deliberate and thoughtful dissemination of relevant data, insights and updates to stakeholders within an organisation. This approach aims to foster transparency, alignment and informed decision-making across all levels of the organisation. By strategically sharing information, leaders can empower their teams with the knowledge they need to understand the organisation's goals, challenges and priorities. This not only cultivates a sense of ownership and accountability but also promotes collaboration and innovation as individuals are equipped to contribute meaningfully to the organisation's success. Moreover, strategic sharing of information helps build trust and credibility among stakeholders, leading to stronger relationships and a more cohesive organisational culture.

Accessible Leadership

Accessible leadership is a frequently discussed concept in schools nationwide, often mentioned alongside phrases like 'non-negotiable' and 'zero-tolerance approach'. However, achieving accessible leadership consistently can be challenging. While 'zero-tolerance' approaches may not always be effective and there are times when negotiation is necessary, it is also important to recognise that leaders cannot always keep their doors open. Realism is key in approaching this concept. Being accessible does not mean never avoiding distractions; rather, it involves fostering a culture where leadership is approachable and available to support everyone in the school community.

Leaders must actively cultivate an atmosphere where teachers feel comfortable reaching out for assistance or guidance whenever needed. One prime example of accessible leadership is Sir Alex Ferguson, the legendary manager of Manchester United. Despite his status as one of the most successful football managers in history, Ferguson was renowned for his approachability and willingness to engage with his players and staff on a personal level. He maintained an open-door policy, not merely as a formal protocol but as a genuine invitation for communication and collaboration. This accessibility enabled Ferguson to build strong relationships with his team members, earning their trust and respect. He knew the reception staff like he knew the chairman. He remembered birthdays. He wrote letters to other players and managers celebrating success and commiserating loss. He had a glass of wine with managers after games whether they lost or won (they often won!). He was, in other aspects, hard and ruthless, but those who worked with him and alongside him always recognised his accessible style. Similarly, school leaders can emulate this approach by fostering an environment where teachers feel valued, heard and supported. By breaking down barriers to communication and actively encouraging dialogue, leaders can create a culture of openness and mutual respect, ultimately promoting the mental wellbeing of their staff.

In the back of a notebook, in a notes section on your phone or on a sticky on your computer, make a note of interactions and go back to them. If someone tells you about their grandson's football match, check in after they have played. Someone mentions an illness – check in to see if they are OK. I worked with a member of SLT who did this effortlessly. He rang you at the end of a difficult day. There was often a queue of people to see him from all across the school. When you spoke to him, you felt heard. You didn't always agree, but you respected him because you knew the next day you could go back into his office and start again. That's what good leaders do. They make people feel comfortable.

IT Systems

At one point, we were using SIMS, EduLink, CPOMs, SISRA, ALPs Connect, Blue Sky, Mint Seating and ParentPay. Remembering your logins, what went where and how to use each one became a major contributor to poor staff wellbeing. Poor IT systems can be a significant source of frustration and inefficiency in schools. Many educational institutions find themselves bogged down by a multitude of disparate systems that create confusion and stress for both staff and students. These outdated and convoluted systems often hinder productivity rather than enhancing it. Instead of empowering educators and administrators, they serve as barriers to effective teaching and learning.

Streamlining IT systems is essential to alleviate these challenges and improve overall efficiency. Schools should undertake a comprehensive review of their existing systems, identifying redundancies and areas for improvement. This process involves not only evaluating the technical aspects of the systems but also considering the user experience and impact on staff wellbeing. Key in this is speaking to the end users and thinking about those who use the systems not as regularly as you do. SLT sometimes live and die by IT systems, but for staff it is an inconvenience in a busy day.

Amalgamating systems and adopting a unified approach can help simplify workflows and reduce the burden on staff. By working collaboratively with teachers and administrators, schools can identify the most effective solutions tailored to their specific needs. This approach promotes buy-in from staff members and ensures that the chosen IT systems align with their preferences and working styles.

Moreover, investing in modern and user-friendly IT solutions can have a transformative effect on school operations. By embracing intuitive platforms and technologies, schools can enhance communication, streamline administrative tasks and facilitate more effective teaching and learning experiences. This not only improves staff morale but also enhances the overall learning environment for students.

In stripping back unnecessary IT systems and prioritising simplicity and usability, schools can create a more efficient and harmonious working environment. It's time to challenge the status quo and embrace IT solutions that empower educators and support staff wellbeing.

Microsoft Teams

A study conducted in the latter part of 2020 within the NHS in North-West England offers valuable insights into the effects of over-communication, particularly through IT systems like Microsoft Teams (UCLan, 2020). This case study sheds light on the dual impact of Teams on staff wellbeing and team dynamics within healthcare settings. While the use of Teams has expanded communication channels, facilitating patient discussions and collaboration among healthcare professionals, it has also raised concerns about the loss of interpersonal connections inherent in face-to-face interactions. Despite the convenience of virtual meetings, many staff members expressed a preference for the personal touch of in-person discussions and advocated for a return to some degree of face-to-face interaction.

Relying solely on written messages poses significant risks, akin to the sentiment expressed in the often-heard complaint, 'This should have been a conversation'. Unlike face-to-face or verbal communication, written messages lack the nuances of tone of voice, facial expressions and body language that are essential for conveying meaning accurately. Without these cues, it becomes challenging to discern the intended tone or gauge the emotional context of the message. As a result, misunderstandings can easily arise, leading to misinterpretations, hurt feelings and damaged relationships.

Furthermore, written communication lacks the immediacy and responsiveness of real-time conversations. While messages can be sent and received quickly, the back-and-forth exchange of ideas that occurs in a conversation allows for immediate clarification and feedback. In contrast, written messages often require additional rounds of correspondence to clarify misunderstandings or address questions, leading to delays and inefficiencies.

Moreover, the brevity and informality of written messages can sometimes lead to miscommunication or ambiguity. In the absence of vocal inflections or visual cues, it can be challenging to convey complex ideas or subtle nuances effectively. As a result, messages may be misunderstood or misinterpreted, leading to confusion or frustration among recipients.

Team messages can also be the killers of productivity, popping up and ruining independent thought. Equally, the absence of incidental learning opportunities, such as casual corridor conversations, can further exacerbate feelings of disconnection among some staff members. Sometimes, getting up to see someone, while taking longer, can lead to better conversations and deeper thinking than a Teams message could ever evoke. Hence, educating staff on what should and shouldn't be communicated via written messages versus face-to-face conversations is crucial for fostering effective communication and preventing misunderstandings.

Communication Policy

Implementing a communication policy that establishes designated hours for messaging can significantly contribute to staff wellbeing. By setting boundaries around when messages can be sent and received, employees are given the opportunity to disconnect and recharge outside of working hours. This practice helps prevent burnout and ensures that staff have dedicated time for rest and personal activities, ultimately improving overall mental health and work–life balance. Additionally, a communication policy fosters a culture of respect for personal time and boundaries among team members, promoting a healthier and more sustainable work environment.

There are several examples of businesses that have implemented communication policies to limit messaging outside of working hours. One notable example is Volkswagen, which introduced a policy in 2011 that disables email communication on employees' smartphones after working hours. This initiative aimed to promote a better work–life balance and reduce stress among employees by preventing them from feeling obligated to respond to work-related emails during their personal time. Similarly, Daimler, another automotive company, implemented a similar policy called 'Mail on Holiday', which allows employees to set their email to automatically delete incoming messages while they are on vacation (Gibson, 2014). These examples demonstrate how organisations can prioritise employee wellbeing by establishing clear boundaries around communication outside of working hours.

Data

Data collection can be a significant source of stress for staff if not managed effectively, especially if you teach multiple year groups. While data can provide valuable insights and inform decision-making processes, it's crucial to consider the timing and purpose of data collection initiatives. Collaboration with staff is essential to ensure that data collection aligns with curriculum maps, school calendars and other organisational priorities. By involving staff in the planning process, schools can identify the most relevant data points and streamline the collection process, making it as seamless and non-disruptive as possible. Time can be built into meetings to input data or, more impactfully, department/staff meetings can be focused on allowing staff time to action it. Giving staff 20 minutes to update and annotate seating plans is a small amount of time but can have a big impact.

Moreover, transparency regarding the purpose of data collection is vital for maintaining trust and buy-in from staff. School leaders should communicate clearly with staff about why certain data is being collected and how it will be used to inform educational practices and improve student outcomes. Providing regular updates and feedback on the outcomes of data analysis can also help staff understand the value of their contributions and feel more engaged in the process.

An excellent example of effective data management can be seen in companies like Google. While Google is known for its extensive use of data analytics to drive decision-making, the company also prioritises employee wellbeing by promoting a healthy work–life balance and fostering a supportive work environment. Google collects vast amounts of data on user behaviour, market trends and internal operations, but also emphasises the importance of qualitative feedback and human intuition in decision-making processes. This balanced approach to data utilisation allows Google to leverage the power of data while also prioritising employee satisfaction and wellbeing. Similarly, schools can adopt a holistic approach to data collection and utilisation, incorporating staff input and feedback to ensure that data initiatives support rather than detract from staff wellbeing.

Parents' Evenings

Research conducted by the Education Endowment Foundation (EEF), a leading independent charity dedicated to breaking the link between family income and educational achievement, has examined the effectiveness of parental engagement strategies, including parents' evenings.

One study funded by the EEF (2021) investigated the impact of different types of parental engagement on students' academic attainment. The study found that parents' evenings, when used in conjunction with other forms of parental engagement such as workshops and newsletters, can lead to small but positive improvements in students' academic outcomes. However, the study also highlighted the importance of ensuring that parents' evenings are well organised, accessible to all parents and focused on meaningful discussions about student progress and support. This last part is key. How many schools provide CPD on effective parents' evenings? How to have an impactful conversation? How many teachers dread parents' evening because they are not well organised or there is potential for parent conflict?

Teachers often feel pressure to provide thorough and informative feedback to parents within a limited timeframe during parents' evenings. This pressure is compounded by the need to address parents' concerns and questions while maintaining a professional demeanour. Additionally, teachers may experience anxiety about delivering potentially challenging feedback to parents, particularly if a student is struggling academically or behaviourally.

Furthermore, the logistics of organising and managing parents' evenings can add to teachers' stress levels. From scheduling appointments to preparing documentation and resources for each meeting, teachers must invest considerable time and effort into planning these events. The demanding nature of parents' evenings can lead to increased workload and feelings of overwhelm among teachers.

Despite the stress associated with parents' evenings, their importance in facilitating meaningful communication between teachers and parents cannot be overstated. Therefore, it is essential for schools to implement strategies to support teachers during these events, such as providing adequate preparation time, offering training on effective communication techniques and fostering a supportive and collaborative school culture. The means of delivery should also be considered. Can they be online, and if not all, could some be via Teams or Zoom? If they are virtual, what are the protocols to address difficult parents? Having a clear policy is really important.

Report Writing

Report writing can be stressful for teachers for several reasons. First, writing comprehensive and accurate reports requires a significant amount of time and effort, often involving the careful review of students' work, assessment data and behavioural observations. Teachers must also consider the individual needs and progress of each student when crafting personalised comments, which can be challenging, especially in larger class sizes.

Moreover, the responsibility of providing constructive feedback to students and their families adds to the pressure of report writing. Teachers aim to strike a balance between highlighting students' achievements and addressing areas for improvement in a manner that is informative and supportive. This task becomes particularly daunting when addressing sensitive topics or delivering potentially challenging feedback.

Additionally, the deadline-driven nature of report writing can exacerbate stress for teachers. Schools typically have set deadlines for submitting reports, leaving teachers with limited time to complete this task alongside their regular teaching duties and other responsibilities. This time pressure can lead to feelings of overwhelm and frustration, especially when teachers are already managing a heavy workload.

Furthermore, the emotional investment that teachers have in their students' progress and success can contribute to the stress of report writing. Teachers often feel a sense of responsibility for accurately capturing students' strengths and areas for development in their reports, knowing that these documents play a significant role in informing parents and shaping students' future academic endeavours.

Evidence regarding the impact of report writing on teachers' stress levels is limited, but anecdotal reports and surveys suggest that it is a significant source of stress in the profession. Studies have found that teachers commonly experience high levels of stress and workload associated with report writing, which can have negative consequences for their overall job satisfaction, mental health and wellbeing. Additionally, research indicates that excessive workload and time pressures, such as those experienced during report writing periods, are key contributors to teacher burnout and attrition (Reinke et al., 2025).

It is worth considering how reports are written and why. Would it be more beneficial to allow for drop-ins for parents? Could AI be utilised to write the reports if key information is put in? Or could it be scrapped altogether and instead utilise soft opportunities to get parents into school (book looks, curriculum days, school shows, meet the teacher).

Overall, communication is the lifeblood of a thriving school community. By prioritising communication and investing in effective communication strategies, schools can cultivate a supportive and collaborative environment where both staff and students can thrive.

Conclusion

In this chapter, we've delved into the profound impact that communication can have on the wellbeing of staff within schools. Drawing on examples from both education and other sectors, it's clear that open, transparent and consistent communication is fundamental to fostering trust, collaboration and a positive working environment. Whether it's in staff meetings, through feedback mechanisms or leadership styles that prioritise listening, effective communication builds the foundation for a supportive school culture.

One key takeaway is that communication must be intentional and strategic. From ensuring that staff feel heard and valued, to offering them platforms for feedback and honest dialogue, schools that prioritise communication are better equipped to create environments where educators can thrive. In contrast, a lack of communication – or ineffective communication – can lead to misunderstandings, feelings of isolation and burnout.

Moreover, leadership plays a crucial role in setting the tone for communication within a school. Leaders who are accessible, who listen more than they speak, and who create structures for regular feedback foster a culture where collaboration and wellbeing are prioritised. This also extends to the way information is shared; decisions made by senior leadership must be communicated clearly and strategically, ensuring staff are engaged and informed every step of the way.

As schools navigate complex challenges, from managing workloads to improving wellbeing, communication remains the constant tool that brings everyone together. The more we invest in clear, thoughtful and inclusive communication, the more we can build resilient teams who feel supported and empowered in their roles.

Reflective Questions

1. **How do you currently communicate with staff to ensure their concerns and ideas are heard?** Reflect on whether there are sufficient opportunities for staff to give feedback and how responsive leadership is to that feedback.
2. **Do your staff meetings foster collaboration and dialogue?** Consider whether your meetings are structured to encourage meaningful contributions from all staff members, and if there is room for creative exchange rather than top-down directives.
3. **Is there a balance between written communication and face-to-face conversations?** Reflect on the mix of communication methods in your setting. Are important conversations happening in person, or are they being relegated to emails or team messages that may lack nuance?
4. **How accessible is your leadership team?** Do staff feel comfortable approaching senior leaders with concerns or suggestions?

What structures are in place to ensure leadership remains open and approachable?
5. **Are feedback mechanisms in your school effective?** Reflect on whether there are channels in place that allow staff to provide anonymous feedback if needed, and if that feedback is acted upon in a transparent way.

References and Further Reading

Anderson, C. (2015). *Mastering the Art of Feedback: Strategies for Success in School Leadership*. Corwin Press.

Blanchard, K., & Johnson, S. (2003). *The One-Minute Manager*. HarperCollins.

Cohen, D. J., & Bradford, D. L. (2005). *Influence Without Authority*. John Wiley & Sons.

Education Endowment Foundation (EEF). (2021). 'Parental engagement: Moderate impact for very low cost based on extensive evidence.' Education Endowment Foundation. https://educationendowmentfoundation.org.uk/education-evidence/teaching-learning-toolkit/parental-engagement

Gibson, M. (2014). 'Here's a Radical Way to End Vacation Email Overload.' *Time*. https://time.com/3116424/daimler-vacation-email-out-of-offic

Goleman, D. (2000). *Emotional Intelligence: Why It Can Matter More Than IQ*. Bantam Books.

Kegan, R., & Lahey, L. L. (2009). *Immunity to Change: How to Overcome It and Unlock the Potential in Yourself and Your Organization*. Harvard Business Press.

Lencioni, P. (2002). *The Five Dysfunctions of a Team: A Leadership Fable*. Jossey-Bass.

Mayer, J. D., Salovey, P., & Caruso, D. R. (2004). 'Emotional Intelligence: Theory, Findings, and Implications.' *Psychological Inquiry*, 15(3), 197–215. www.jstor.org/stable/20447229

Mulally, A. (2012). *American Icon: Alan Mulally and the Fight to Save Ford Motor Company*. Penguin Press.

Nadella, S. (2017). *Hit Refresh: The Quest to Rediscover Microsoft's Soul and Imagine a Better Future for Everyone*. Harper Business.

Nooyi, I. (2018). *My Life in Full: Work, Family, and Our Future*. Portfolio.

Reinke, W. M., Herman, K. C., Stormont, M., & Ghasemi, F. (2025). 'Teacher stress, coping, burnout, and plans to leave the field: A post-pandemic survey.' *School Mental Health*, 17, 32–44. https://link.springer.com/content/pdf/10.1007/s12310-024-09738-7.pdf

Robinson, D., Perryman, S., & Hayday, S. (2004). *The Drivers of Employee Engagement*. Report for the Institute for Employment Studies. www.employment-studies.co.uk/system/files/resources/files/408.pdf

Senge, P. M. (2006). *The Fifth Discipline: The Art and Practice of the Learning Organization.* Doubleday.

UCLan. (2020). 'Microsoft Teams – Understanding the impact the introduction of Microsoft Teams has had on team performance in response to the COVID-19 pandemic within the East Lancashire Intensive Home Support Service.' https://clok.uclan.ac.uk/40642

Brown, E. (2011). 'Volkswagen turns off email for BlackBerry workers.' ZDNET. www.zdnet.com/article/volkswagen-turns-off-email-for-blackberry-workers

Chapter 6
Appreciation

In the realm of elite sports, recognition is more than just a pat on the back – it's a driving force that can elevate an athlete's performance from good to legendary. Consider Megan Rapinoe, a celebrated player for the US Women's National Soccer Team. Beyond her exceptional talent, what fuelled her relentless drive was the appreciation she received from her coaches, teammates and fans. This recognition validated her hard work, reinforced her value to the team and propelled her to push her limits further each day. Rapinoe's journey is a testament to how appreciation can inspire excellence and resilience, driving individuals to achieve greatness.

Now, let's pivot to the world of business. At Zappos, a company renowned for its exceptional employee recognition programmes, appreciation is deeply woven into the corporate fabric. Employees are celebrated not just for their successes but also for their efforts and innovative ideas, even if they don't always lead to immediate results. For instance, Zappos has a peer-to-peer recognition programme where employees can acknowledge each other's contributions through a system of points that can be redeemed for rewards. Additionally, the company hosts regular events to celebrate milestones and achievements, fostering a culture of appreciation and motivation.

So, what can schools learn from these examples? Imagine a school environment where teachers and support staff are regularly and genuinely appreciated for their contributions. Picture a place where every effort, big or small, is acknowledged and valued. This is not just a utopian vision but a realistic goal that can have a profound impact on staff wellbeing. In this chapter, we will explore the transformative power of appreciation within the school setting, drawing lessons from the worlds of business and sport.

Appreciation, when practised authentically and consistently, can become the bedrock of a positive school culture. It can enhance morale, reduce stress and build a strong, cohesive community. Just as Megan Rapinoe thrived on the appreciation of her supporters, and Zappos employees innovate within a culture of recognition, school staff can reach new heights when they feel truly valued. Through practical examples and actionable strategies, this chapter will guide you on how to cultivate a culture of appreciation in your school, unlocking the potential for a happier, more engaged, and more effective educational team.

💡 Insights from Jake Humphries and Professor Damian Hughes

In the realm of high performance, few texts are as enlightening as *High Performance* by Jake Humphries and Professor Damian Hughes (2021). This book dives deep into the psyche of elite performers across various fields, revealing the crucial elements that distinguish the best from the rest. One of the most striking takeaways from their exploration is the undeniable impact of genuine appreciation on individual and team performance.

Humphries and Hughes argue that high-performing teams are not just about talent or strategy; they are fundamentally about people. At the core of their success lies a culture of recognition and gratitude. They highlight stories of athletes and teams who, despite their undeniable skills, struggled until they embraced a culture of mutual appreciation. For instance, the All Blacks, New Zealand's legendary rugby team, are renowned not just for their athletic prowess but for their deep sense of connection and respect for each other. This culture of appreciation is so ingrained that it shapes every interaction and decision within the team, fostering an environment where every player feels valued and motivated to contribute their best.

One poignant example from Humphries and Hughes's work is the story of the British Cycling team. Under the leadership of Sir Dave Brailsford, they transformed from a struggling squad into one of the most dominant forces in cycling history. Brailsford's philosophy was simple yet profound: every tiny improvement, every ounce of effort and every act of appreciation mattered. The team's success was not just a result of strategic training but of a relentless focus on recognising and celebrating the contributions of each member. Whether it was a mechanic who fine-tuned a bike or a coach who developed a new training method, everyone's role was crucial, and their efforts were consistently acknowledged. This culture of appreciation, according to Humphries and Hughes, created a ripple effect of motivation and excellence that propelled the team to unprecedented heights.

In the context of schools, this principle translates seamlessly. Imagine a staff room where every teacher, every janitor and every administrative staff member is recognised for their unique contributions. Picture the impact of a principal who, like Sir Dave Brailsford, takes the time to acknowledge the small yet significant efforts of each team member. This culture of appreciation not only boosts morale but also fosters a sense of belonging and purpose. When staff feel genuinely valued, their engagement and commitment soar, creating a positive feedback loop that enhances overall school performance.

A Lesson from Business: The Ritz-Carlton's Approach to Appreciation

In the world of luxury hospitality, few brands are as synonymous with excellence as The Ritz-Carlton. Known for its impeccable service and attention to detail, The Ritz-Carlton has built its reputation on a foundation of appreciation and recognition, not only for its guests but also for its employees. The company's philosophy, encapsulated in its Gold Standards, underscores the importance of recognising and valuing the contributions of every team member.

One of the most compelling aspects of The Ritz-Carlton's approach is their daily 'Line-Up'. Every day, at every location worldwide, employees gather for a short meeting where they share success stories, recognise outstanding performance and reinforce the company's core values. This practice is not just about communication; it is a powerful tool for fostering a culture of appreciation. By consistently highlighting and celebrating the efforts of their staff, The Ritz-Carlton ensures that employees feel valued and motivated.

A notable example of this practice in action is the story of Joshie the Giraffe. A young guest left his beloved stuffed giraffe, Joshie, at a Ritz-Carlton hotel. When the hotel staff found Joshie, they didn't just return him; they went above and beyond to create a memorable experience. They took photos of Joshie enjoying various amenities of the hotel – getting a massage at the spa, lounging by the pool and even working in the security office. These photos were sent back with the giraffe, accompanied by a letter detailing Joshie's extended vacation.

This extraordinary gesture, driven by the staff's appreciation of the opportunity to make a guest happy, exemplifies The Ritz-Carlton's commitment to recognition and value. It wasn't just about pleasing a guest; it was about recognising the importance of small acts and celebrating the employees who go the extra mile. The story of Joshie the Giraffe went viral, becoming a testament to the power of appreciation and its ripple effects on employee motivation and customer satisfaction.

Translating this to a school setting, imagine a principal or school leader who adopts a similar approach. By holding regular meetings where staff achievements are highlighted and celebrated, leaders can create an environment where appreciation becomes a norm. Whether it's a teacher who stayed late to help a struggling student, a cleaner who ensured the hallways were spotless or a receptionist who dealt with a difficult parent, recognising these efforts can have a profound impact.

Creating a culture of appreciation in schools can involve simple yet effective practices such as a 'Staff Shout-Out' board where colleagues can post notes of thanks and recognition, monthly awards for outstanding contributions, or personalised thank-you notes from leadership. These practices, inspired by The Ritz-Carlton's example, can transform the school environment, making it a place where every staff member feels valued and motivated to contribute their best.

Implementing a Culture of Appreciation: Strategies and Tools for School Leaders

Building a culture of appreciation in schools requires intentionality and consistent effort. By incorporating specific strategies and tools, school leaders can create an environment where staff feel recognised, valued and motivated. Below are actionable steps that can help foster a culture of appreciation in educational settings.

Daily or Weekly Recognition Routines

Inspired by The Ritz-Carlton's daily 'Line-Up', schools can implement regular recognition routines. These can take the form of daily morning briefings or weekly staff meetings where achievements, big and small, are highlighted.

- **Morning huddles:** Start the day with a brief meeting where staff members share positive news and acknowledge each other's efforts. This sets a

positive tone for the day and reinforces a culture of appreciation. These huddles can be structured with a few key components:
- **Opening gratitude:** Begin with a moment where staff can express gratitude for specific colleagues or events. This might include thanking a teacher for covering a class or a staff member who organised a successful event.
- **Success stories:** Allow time for sharing success stories from the classroom or extracurricular activities. This could involve discussing a student's significant improvement, a successful lesson plan or the completion of a challenging project.
- **Encouragement and support:** Conclude with words of encouragement for the day ahead, emphasising teamwork and mutual support.
* **Weekly celebrations:** Dedicate time during weekly staff meetings to recognise outstanding contributions. Encourage team members to share stories of colleagues who went above and beyond. These celebrations can be more detailed:
  - **Themed recognitions:** Each week can have a theme, such as 'Innovation in Teaching', 'Outstanding Support Staff' or 'Excellence in Mentor Time'. This ensures diverse recognition across different roles and achievements.
  - **Peer nominations:** Implement a system where staff can nominate their peers for recognition based on the weekly theme. This can be done anonymously to encourage honest and heartfelt nominations.
  - **Certificates and awards:** Present certificates or small awards to those recognised. This adds a formal touch to the appreciation and provides a tangible reminder of their valued contribution.

Staff Shout-Out Boards

Creating a visible, dedicated space for recognition can have a powerful impact.

* **Shout-out board:** Set up a bulletin board in the staff room/communal space where employees can post notes of thanks and recognition. This encourages peer-to-peer appreciation and allows everyone to see the positive contributions being made. To enhance this:

- **Structured posting:** Provide templates or sticky notes with prompts such as 'Thank you for...' or 'Great job on...'. This helps staff articulate their appreciation clearly and thoughtfully.
- **Rotating highlights:** Each week, highlight different shout-outs by moving them to a central spot on the board. This ensures all recognitions are prominently displayed and appreciated by the entire staff.
- **Remove and replace:** These boards quickly lose their impact if they are allowed to go stale. Make it dynamic and ever-changing. Make it part of someone's duty/appraisal (as part of a wider target) to constantly change it. In SLT meetings, go and look at it and add your own. Make it matter.
- **Digital shout-outs:** Use digital platforms, such as an internal website, intranet or Teams, to create a virtual shout-out board. This is particularly useful for larger schools.
  - **Interactive features:** Allow staff to 'like' or comment on shout-outs to foster interaction and additional layers of appreciation.
  - **Regular updates:** Appoint a staff member to regularly update the digital board with new shout-outs and ensure it remains an active and engaging space.

Personalised Thank-You Notes

Taking the time to write personalised thank-you notes can have a profound impact on morale.

- **Handwritten notes:** School leaders should regularly write and deliver handwritten notes to staff members, acknowledging their specific contributions and expressing gratitude.
  - **Specific praise:** Ensure that each note includes specific details about the recipient's actions and the positive impact they had. This shows genuine recognition and thoughtfulness.
  - **Regular practice:** Make this a regular practice, perhaps dedicating a specific day each week to writing these notes, or as part of an SLT meeting. This ensures consistent and ongoing appreciation.
- **E-thank yous:** Utilise email/Teams for quick and personalised thank-you messages, ensuring that the recognition is timely and relevant.

- **Timely feedback:** Send e-thank-you notes as soon as possible after the appreciated action. This immediacy reinforces the positive behaviour and shows that it was noticed and valued.
- **Follow-up:** Occasionally follow up on e-thank-you notes with a face-to-face conversation, reiterating the appreciation and building a stronger personal connection.
- **The small matter:** If you visit a member of staff's lesson, perhaps to collect a student or pass on a message, try to spot something good and then follow up after. They may be using a visualiser or cold calling. They equally may have a great display or have a nice attitude with the class. These little things matter and create a positive culture.

Celebrating Milestones

Acknowledging significant milestones in an employee's career can strengthen their connection to the school.

- **Service anniversaries:** Celebrate the anniversaries of staff members' employment. Recognise their years of service during staff meetings and with tokens of appreciation such as certificates or small gifts.
  - **Public recognition:** Announce service anniversaries in staff meetings, newsletters and school assemblies. This public recognition enhances the sense of achievement.
  - **Personalised gifts:** Offer personalised gifts that reflect the individual's interests or contributions. For example, a custom-made plaque, a gift card to their favourite restaurant or a book related to their professional interests. A nice touch is always something from the year they started – a book which was released that year, a bottle of wine, etc.
- **Personal achievements:** Celebrate personal milestones such as completing a degree, receiving a certification, running a marathon or reaching personal goals. Recognise these achievements publicly to show that you value their personal growth and development.
  - **Spotlight features:** Create spotlight features in the school newsletter or on social media, sharing the personal achievements and stories of staff members. This not only celebrates the individual but also inspires others.

- **Supportive environment:** Encourage a supportive environment where colleagues can share their personal milestones and receive encouragement and recognition from their peers.

Peer Recognition Programmes

Encourage a culture where appreciation is not just top-down but also peer-to-peer.

- **Recognition nominations:** Create a system where staff can nominate their peers for recognition. This can be done through an anonymous nomination box or an online form.
  - **Inclusive criteria:** Ensure that the criteria for nominations are broad and inclusive, allowing all staff members, regardless of their role, to be eligible for recognition.
  - **Regular announcements:** Announce the peer recognitions regularly during staff meetings or through internal communications, highlighting the collaborative and supportive culture of the school.
- **Recognition committees:** Form a committee of staff members who are responsible for overseeing and promoting recognition activities. This can include organising events, collecting nominations and ensuring that recognition is inclusive and comprehensive.
  - **Diverse membership:** Ensure the committee is diverse, representing various roles and departments within the school. This ensures a wide range of perspectives and ideas.
  - **Regular meetings:** Hold regular meetings to plan and review recognition activities, ensuring they are effective and well received. Use these meetings to gather feedback and continually improve the recognition programme.

Public Acknowledgement

Publicly acknowledging staff contributions can enhance their sense of pride and motivation.

- **School assemblies:** Recognise staff achievements during school assemblies, allowing students and the wider school community to see and appreciate the contributions of staff.

- **Student participation:** Involve students in the recognition process, such as having student representatives present the awards or share testimonials about the positive impact of the staff members being recognised. Have a mentor/form-time activity of writing thank-you cards to staff.
- **Special segments:** Dedicate special segments of the assembly to staff recognition, ensuring it is a prominent and celebrated part of the event.
- **Social media:** Use the school's social media platforms to highlight staff achievements and express public appreciation.
  - **Regular posts:** Make regular posts about staff achievements, using engaging visuals and personal stories to highlight their contributions.
  - **Interactive content:** Encourage the school community to engage with these posts by liking, sharing and commenting. This not only spreads the recognition further but also fosters a positive online community.

Detailed Implementation Plan

To ensure these strategies are effectively implemented, school leaders should develop a structured plan:

1. Assess Current Culture

Conduct surveys or focus groups to understand the current state of staff appreciation and identify areas for improvement.

- **Anonymous surveys:** Use anonymous surveys to gather honest feedback from staff about their experiences and perceptions of appreciation within the school. Include questions about the frequency and quality of recognition they receive.
- **Focus groups:** Organise focus groups with representatives from different roles and departments to discuss the current culture and brainstorm ideas for improvement. This qualitative approach can provide deeper insights and specific examples.

Top Tip for Effective Staff Feedback

Consider very carefully when you ask for staff feedback and what questions you ask. I've encountered countless poorly designed surveys that fail to provide meaningful insights. To ensure your feedback process is effective:

- **Highlight previous actions:** Begin by emphasising the changes and improvements made based on the last survey. This shows staff that their input is valued and acted upon, encouraging more thoughtful and honest responses.
- **Timing is key:** Choose the timing of your survey carefully. Avoid distributing surveys at the end of a busy term, as responses may be influenced by fatigue and stress. Instead, select a period when staff are more likely to provide constructive and reflective feedback.

By following these tips, you can create a feedback process that genuinely supports staff wellbeing and continuous improvement.

2. Set Clear Goals

Define what you want to achieve with your appreciation initiatives. Goals might include improving staff morale, increasing retention rates or fostering a more collaborative environment.

- **SMART goals:** Set SMART (Specific, Measurable, Achievable, Relevant, Time-bound) goals for your appreciation initiatives. For example: 'Increase the frequency of peer-to-peer recognitions by 50 per cent within six months.'
- **Action plan:** Develop an action plan outlining the specific steps needed to achieve these goals. Assign responsibilities and set deadlines to ensure accountability.

3. Create a Recognition Calendar

Develop a recognition calendar to plan and schedule regular appreciation activities throughout the school year.

- **Annual overview:** Create an annual overview of key appreciation events and activities, ensuring a balanced distribution throughout the year. Add this to your SLT meetings so that they aren't missed, and everyone is held accountable for implementing them.
- **Monthly themes:** Designate monthly themes for recognition, such as 'Teamwork', 'Innovation' or 'Dedication'. This provides a structured approach and ensures various aspects of staff contributions are highlighted.

- **Integration with school events:** Integrate appreciation activities with existing school events and milestones, such as the end of term celebrations, staff meetings or inset days.

4. Engage Staff

Involve staff in the planning process. Their input can provide valuable insights and ensure that the initiatives resonate with everyone.

- **Suggestion box:** Implement a suggestion box, both physical and digital, where staff can submit ideas for recognition activities and improvements.
- **Recognition task force:** Form a recognition task force composed of volunteers from various roles and departments. This group can provide ongoing input and help implement the recognition initiatives.

5. Monitor and Adjust

Regularly review the effectiveness of the appreciation strategies. Gather feedback and make adjustments as necessary to keep the initiatives fresh and impactful.

- **Feedback mechanisms:** Use surveys and focus groups periodically to gather feedback on the recognition initiatives. Ask specific questions about what is working well and what could be improved.
- **Data analysis:** Analyse data such as retention rates, absenteeism and staff satisfaction surveys to assess the impact of the recognition programmes.
- **Continuous improvement:** Based on feedback and data analysis, make necessary adjustments to the recognition strategies. This could include introducing new activities, discontinuing less effective ones or refining existing practices.

Real-Life Examples of Effective Appreciation Strategies

Example 1: Morning Huddles at Seattle Children's Hospital

Seattle Children's Hospital uses morning huddles as part of its commitment to effective communication and teamwork. Morning huddles are short, focused meetings where team members can share updates, express gratitude and align on daily goals.

- **Gratitude round:** Each huddle starts with a gratitude round, where team members express thanks for specific actions by their colleagues. This practice boosts morale and fosters a supportive atmosphere.
- **Success stories:** Staff share success stories from their recent work, highlighting innovative approaches, patient successes and collaborative efforts.
- **Encouraging quotes:** The huddle concludes with an encouraging quote or message from a team leader, setting a positive tone for the day.

For more information on this practice, see:

- *Lean Hospitals: Improving Quality, Patient Safety, and Employee Engagement* by Mark Graban (2012).

Example 2: Monthly Awards at Patagonia

Patagonia, the outdoor clothing company, is well known for its commitment to employee appreciation and recognition.

- **Employee of the Month:** Staff nominate their peers for the Employee of the Month award. The recipient is featured in the company newsletter and receives a personalised plaque.
- **Themed awards:** Patagonia recognises diverse contributions with awards such as 'Innovative Designer' and 'Community Champion'. Each award comes with a unique trophy and a small gift voucher.
- **Celebration events:** Award ceremonies are held during staff meetings, creating a celebratory atmosphere. Detailed profiles of the awardees are shared, highlighting their achievements and impact.

Example 3: Personalised Thank-You Notes at Southwest Airlines

Southwest Airlines' former CEO, Herb Kelleher, and current CEO, Gary Kelly, are known for their practice of sending personalised thank-you notes to employees.

- **Handwritten notes:** Leaders at Southwest Airlines write handwritten notes to staff members, detailing specific actions and their positive impacts. This personal touch has significantly boosted staff morale and engagement.
- **E-thank yous:** In addition to handwritten notes, Southwest Airlines uses email for quick and personalised thank-you messages, ensuring timely and thoughtful recognition.

By implementing these strategies and drawing inspiration from successful case studies, school leaders can create a thriving culture of appreciation. This not only enhances staff wellbeing but also contributes to a more positive, supportive and effective educational environment. As we continue to explore the CAGE approach, the next chapter will delve into the importance of Growth and Development, providing further insights into fostering a holistic approach to staff wellbeing in schools.

Potential Pitfalls of Appreciation Programmes

While appreciation programmes can significantly boost morale and foster a positive culture, they are not without their potential pitfalls. School leaders should be aware of these challenges to ensure that their appreciation efforts are genuinely effective and inclusive.

Inconsistency and Perceived Favouritism

One major pitfall of appreciation programmes is inconsistency, which can lead to perceptions of favouritism. When recognition is not applied uniformly, it can create divisions among staff and undermine the programme's overall effectiveness.

 Insights from General Motors

General Motors faced criticism when their employee recognition programme was perceived as inconsistent. Some employees felt that recognition was based more on favouritism than on actual performance, leading to decreased morale and increased resentment among staff.

Strategies to Avoid Inconsistency and Favouritism

- **Transparent criteria:** Establish clear, transparent criteria for recognition to ensure that all staff understand what behaviours and achievements are being rewarded.
- **Regular training:** Provide training for those involved in the recognition process to ensure they apply criteria consistently.
- **Broad participation:** Encourage a wide range of staff members to participate in the nomination and selection process to mitigate bias.

Superficial or Insincere Recognition

Appreciation must be genuine and meaningful. Superficial or insincere recognition can be counterproductive, making employees feel undervalued and distrustful of the programme.

Insights from United Airlines

United Airlines faced backlash when it replaced quarterly performance bonuses with a lottery system that rewarded a small number of employees with significant prizes. This move was widely criticised as it seemed to undermine genuine appreciation and instead made recognition feel like a gamble (Gibson, 2018).

Strategies to Ensure Genuine Recognition

- **Specific praise:** Ensure that recognition is specific and detailed, highlighting the particular actions and impacts of the individual's contributions.
- **Personal touch:** Where possible, add a personal element to the recognition, such as a handwritten note or a face-to-face conversation.
- **Consistent feedback:** Combine public recognition with regular, private feedback to show ongoing appreciation and support.

Overemphasis on Individual Achievements

While individual recognition is important, overemphasis on personal achievements can create unhealthy competition and detract from the importance of teamwork and collaboration.

Insights From Wells Fargo

Wells Fargo's aggressive sales goals and reward system led to a scandal where employees opened unauthorised accounts to meet targets. The focus on individual sales achievements created a toxic culture and undermined ethical behaviour and teamwork.

Strategies to Promote Teamwork and Collaboration

- **Team awards:** Include team-based recognition in the programme to celebrate collaborative efforts and group achievements.
- **Balanced recognition:** Ensure that the recognition programme highlights both individual and team accomplishments equally.
- **Collaborative goals:** Set and reward collaborative goals that require teamwork to achieve, reinforcing the importance of working together.

Ignoring Diverse Contributions

Recognition programmes can inadvertently overlook the contributions of certain staff members, especially those in less visible roles. This can lead to feelings of neglect and inequality.

Lack of Follow-Through

Appreciation programmes can lose credibility if there is a lack of follow-through on promised rewards or if recognised efforts do not lead to tangible support and development.

Strategies for Effective Follow-Through

- **Meaningful rewards:** Ensure that recognition is accompanied by meaningful rewards, such as professional development opportunities, additional resources or career advancement support.
- **Action plans:** Develop action plans for recognised employees to help them continue their growth and contributions.

- **Consistent review:** Regularly review and update the recognition programme to ensure it remains relevant and effective in meeting staff needs.

By being aware of these potential pitfalls and implementing strategies to address them, school leaders can create robust appreciation programmes that truly enhance staff wellbeing and foster a positive, inclusive culture.

Appreciation from the Start: Building a Culture of Recognition from Day One

The foundation of a strong appreciation culture is laid the moment a new staff member joins the school. The induction phase is critical in shaping their initial impressions, building their engagement, and integrating them into the school's community. When new employees feel valued and appreciated from the start, they are more likely to become motivated, committed and productive members of the team. Here are strategies to ensure that appreciation begins on day one.

Welcoming New Staff with Open Arms

A warm and genuine welcome sets the tone for a new staff member's experience. This initial phase should not only be about providing necessary information but also about making new employees feel valued and included.

Personalised Welcome Packages

Provide new employees with personalised welcome packages that include not only essential items like school handbooks and schedules but also thoughtful gifts such as school-branded merchandise, personalised notes from the principal or colleagues and a list of resources and support available to them.

> **Google's 'Noogler' Welcome Package: A Deep Dive**
>
> Google's onboarding process, celebrated for its inclusivity and engagement, exemplifies how a well-designed welcome package can create

a positive and impactful first impression. This approach not only introduces new hires – known as 'Nooglers' – to the company but also embeds them into the culture from day one. Here's an in-depth look at what makes Google's welcome package particularly effective.

1. Personalised Welcome Items

Google's welcome package is designed to make new hires feel immediately valued and connected to the company. It typically includes:

- **Branded berchandise:** Each Noogler receives Google-branded items such as T-shirts, mugs, notebooks and backpacks. These items serve both practical and symbolic purposes. The branded merchandise helps new employees feel like part of the Google family and creates a sense of pride and belonging.
- **Customised gear:** The package often includes customised gear that reflects the new hire's department or role, adding a personal touch and helping them feel more integrated into their specific team.

2. Personal Welcome Letter

A personal welcome letter from a senior leader, such as the CEO or a relevant department head, is a key component of the welcome package:

- **Warm greeting:** The letter provides a warm and sincere greeting, expressing excitement about the new hire joining the team. This personalised communication reinforces the value the company places on the new employee.
- **Company vision and values:** The letter typically outlines Google's vision, values and culture, offering insights into what makes the company unique. This helps new hires understand the broader context of their role and how they contribute to the company's mission.

3. Comprehensive Resource Guide

The welcome package includes a comprehensive resource guide designed to help new hires navigate their new role and environment:

- **Employee handbook:** This handbook covers essential information about company policies, benefits and procedures. It acts as a go-to reference for understanding the day-to-day operations and expectations at Google.
- **Onboarding schedule:** New hires receive a detailed onboarding schedule that outlines the training sessions, meet-and-greets and initial projects they will be involved in. This helps them plan their first few weeks and sets clear expectations.
- **Role-specific resources:** Depending on their role, new hires may receive additional resources such as training materials, access to specific tools and information about ongoing projects. This targeted information helps them hit the ground running and feel prepared for their new responsibilities.

4. *Integration into Company Culture*

Google's welcome package is not just about logistics but also about cultural integration:

- **Cultural symbols:** The package includes items and messages that reflect Google's unique culture, such as references to the company's innovation, diversity, and inclusivity initiatives. This helps new hires connect with the company's ethos and feel aligned with its values.
- **Social integration:** New hires are encouraged to participate in team-building activities and social events. The welcome package often includes invitations to these events, fostering early engagement and helping them build relationships with their colleagues.

5. *Feedback and Follow-Up*

Google places a strong emphasis on feedback and follow-up to ensure that new hires feel continuously supported:

- **Feedback channels:** New hires are encouraged to provide feedback on their onboarding experience through various channels. This feedback helps Google refine its onboarding process and address any potential issues.

- **Check-ins:** Regular check-ins with managers and HR representatives are scheduled to ensure new employees are adjusting well and to address any concerns they might have. These follow-ups reinforce the company's commitment to their success and wellbeing.

The Impact of Google's Approach

Google's thoughtful and comprehensive welcome package is designed to create a positive first impression and foster a sense of belonging. By combining practical resources with personalised touches and a strong emphasis on cultural integration, Google ensures that new hires feel appreciated and engaged from the outset. This approach not only helps new employees' transition smoothly into their roles but also strengthens their connection to the company's values and goals.

Effective and Supportive Orientation Programmes

Orientation programmes should be comprehensive and supportive, providing new employees with the tools and knowledge they need to succeed while also making them feel welcome and appreciated.

Buddy System

Pair new staff members with a buddy – an experienced colleague who can offer guidance, answer questions and provide social support. This helps new employees feel connected and appreciated from the start.

Microsoft's Onboarding Buddy Program: A Comprehensive Overview

Microsoft's Onboarding Buddy Program is a well-structured initiative designed to support new employees as they integrate into the company. This programme pairs new hires with experienced employees, known as 'buddies', who offer guidance and support throughout the initial months of employment. Here's a detailed look at how the programme operates and its impact on new hires.

1. The Role of the Onboarding Buddy

An integral part of the programme is the onboarding buddy, an experienced employee who serves as a mentor and resource for new hires. The role of the buddy includes:

- **Personal introduction:** The buddy meets with the new hire before their official start date to provide an introduction to the company culture, the team and the office environment. This early interaction helps to reduce first-day anxiety and fosters a welcoming atmosphere.
- **Guidance and support:** Throughout the initial months, the buddy offers guidance on navigating Microsoft's systems, processes and organisational structure. This includes helping new hires understand internal tools, departmental procedures and project workflows.
- **Social integration:** The buddy plays a key role in integrating the new hire into the social fabric of the company. This includes introducing them to team members, inviting them to social events and facilitating informal interactions that help build relationships.

2. Structured Onboarding Plan

The buddy programme is supported by a structured onboarding plan that ensures both the buddy and the new hire have clear expectations and goals:

- **Onboarding schedule:** A detailed schedule is provided, outlining key milestones and activities for the new hire's first few months. This includes training sessions, team meetings and one-on-one check-ins with the buddy.
- **Goal-setting:** Specific goals are set for the new hire's initial period, including learning objectives, project assignments and integration milestones. The buddy helps the new hire track their progress and achieve these goals.

3. *Resources and Training for Buddies*

To ensure that buddies are effective in their role, Microsoft provides them with resources and training:

- **Buddy training:** Buddies undergo training to prepare them for their role. This training includes best practices for mentorship, communication skills and how to effectively support new hires.
- **Resource toolkit:** Buddies receive a toolkit with resources such as guidelines on common challenges new hires face, tips for providing feedback and information on Microsoft's culture and values.

4. *Feedback Mechanisms*

Feedback is a crucial component of the buddy programme, both for improving the programme itself and for supporting the new hire's development:

- **Regular check-ins:** Scheduled check-ins are conducted between the new hire, their buddy and their manager. These check-ins provide an opportunity to discuss progress, address any issues and adjust the onboarding plan as needed.
- **Programme feedback:** New hires are encouraged to provide feedback on their experience with the buddy programme. This feedback is used to make continuous improvements and ensure that the programme meets the needs of future new hires.

5. *Impact on New Hires*

Microsoft's Onboarding Buddy Program has several benefits that contribute to the new hire's overall experience:

- **Enhanced integration:** By providing a dedicated point of contact, the programme helps new hires integrate more smoothly into the company culture and feel more connected to their team.
- **Reduced anxiety:** The support from a buddy helps alleviate the common anxieties associated with starting a new job, such as navigating the workplace and understanding company norms.
- **Increased engagement:** New hires who feel supported and valued are more likely to be engaged and motivated. The buddy

> programme fosters a sense of belonging and encourages active participation in the company culture.
>
> 6. *Long-Term Benefits*
>
> The positive effects of the buddy programme extend beyond the initial onboarding period:
>
> - **Employee retention:** Effective onboarding and support contribute to higher employee satisfaction and retention. New hires who have a positive onboarding experience are more likely to stay with the company long-term.
> - **Cultural continuity:** The buddy programem reinforces Microsoft's culture and values by ensuring that new hires receive consistent messaging and support from experienced employees.
>
> **Conclusion**
>
> Microsoft's Onboarding Buddy Program is a prime example of how structured support and mentorship can enhance the onboarding experience for new hires. By pairing new employees with experienced buddies, Microsoft not only helps them navigate their new roles but also fosters a sense of belonging and integration into the company culture. This approach not only eases the transition for new hires but also strengthens their engagement and long-term commitment to the organisation.

Early Recognition and Positive Feedback

From the very beginning, it's crucial to recognise and acknowledge the efforts and contributions of new staff members. Positive feedback and early recognition can significantly impact their morale and motivation.

Immediate Feedback and Encouragement

Provide new employees with immediate and constructive feedback. Celebrate their early successes, no matter how small, to build their confidence and show appreciation for their efforts.

Appreciation

HubSpot's Early Wins Recognition: An In-Depth Look

HubSpot, renowned for its robust approach to employee satisfaction, employs a strategic 'Early Wins Recognition' programme designed to celebrate and acknowledge new hires' early contributions. This initiative underscores the company's commitment to fostering a culture of appreciation and support from the outset. Here's a detailed exploration of how HubSpot's programme functions and its impact on new employees.

1. Celebrating Early Achievements

The core of HubSpot's Early Wins Recognition programme is the emphasis on celebrating new hires' initial successes:

- **Acknowledgement of contributions:** Managers and team members actively recognise and celebrate early achievements, no matter how small. This could include successful completion of initial projects, effective problem-solving or positive feedback from colleagues or clients.
- **Public recognition:** Early wins are often highlighted in team meetings, company-wide newsletters or internal communication channels. This public acknowledegment reinforces the new hire's value and integrates them into the broader team culture.

Example: HubSpot's Monthly Recognition Rituals

HubSpot holds monthly recognition rituals where managers and peers share success stories and celebrate recent achievements. This regular practice ensures that early contributions are noticed and appreciated, fostering a positive and motivating environment.

2. Structured Recognition Process

HubSpot has developed a structured process to ensure that early achievements are effectively recognised:

- **Recognition criteria:** Clear criteria are established for what constitutes an 'early win'. This includes specific performance metrics, successful project milestones or noteworthy contributions to team goals.

- **Feedback and reporting:** Managers and team members are encouraged to provide feedback and report early wins through structured channels. This could include recognition platforms, internal surveys or direct communication with HR.

Example: HubSpot's Recognition Platform

HubSpot uses an internal recognition platform where employees can post shout-outs and commendations. This platform helps track and manage early wins and ensures that no achievements go unnoticed.

3. *Manager and Peer Involvement*

Effective recognition involves both managers and peers, creating a well-rounded support system for new hires:

- **Manager participation:** Managers play a crucial role in identifying and celebrating early wins. They provide feedback, acknowledge successes and encourage new hires by highlighting their contributions in formal and informal settings.
- **Peer contributions:** Peers are also encouraged to recognise and celebrate their colleagues' achievements. This peer-to-peer recognition reinforces a supportive team culture and helps new hires build strong relationships.

Example: Peer Shout-Outs at HubSpot

At HubSpot, peer shout-outs are a common practice where employees can publicly acknowledge their colleagues' contributions. This peer-driven approach helps reinforce a culture of mutual appreciation and support.

4. *Impact on New Hires*

The Early Wins Recognition programme at HubSpot has several key benefits for new employees:

- **Boosted morale:** Early recognition of achievements helps boost new hires' morale and confidence, making them feel valued and supported from the start.
- **Enhanced engagement:** By celebrating early successes, new hires are more likely to feel engaged and motivated, leading to increased productivity and commitment to their role.
- **Positive onboarding experience:** Acknowledging early wins contributes to a positive onboarding experience, which can improve job satisfaction and reduce turnover.

Example: HubSpot's Employee Satisfaction Scores

HubSpot consistently ranks high in employee satisfaction surveys, with its focus on recognition and appreciation being a significant contributing factor. The Early Wins Recognition programme is part of a broader strategy that includes regular feedback and support, which helps maintain high levels of employee engagement and satisfaction.

5. *Long-Term Benefits*

The benefits of early recognition extend beyond the initial onboarding phase:

- **Increased retention:** Recognising early contributions helps new hires feel integrated and valued, which can lead to higher retention rates and lower turnover.
- **Cultural reinforcement:** Early wins recognition reinforces HubSpot's commitment to a culture of appreciation and support, setting a positive tone for the new hires' ongoing experience with the company.
- **Continuous improvement:** The feedback and insights gained from early recognition contribute to continuous improvement in the onboarding process, ensuring that new hires receive the support they need to succeed.

> **Conclusion**
>
> HubSpot's Early Wins Recognition programme exemplifies how strategic acknowledgement of early achievements can foster a supportive and appreciative work environment. By celebrating new hires' initial successes, involving managers and peers, and integrating recognition into the company's culture, HubSpot ensures that new employees feel valued and engaged from day one. This approach not only enhances the onboarding experience but also contributes to long-term employee satisfaction and retention.

Inclusive Team Integration

Ensuring that new employees feel like a valued part of the team from the start is essential for fostering a sense of belonging and appreciation.

Team Introductions and Social Events

Organise introductions and social events to help new staff integrate into the team. This could include informal coffee meetings, team lunches or welcome parties that allow new employees to connect with their colleagues in a relaxed setting.

Mentorship and Professional Development

Provide access to mentorship programmes and professional development opportunities. Encourage new employees to pursue further training and education, showing that their long-term success is important to the school.

> **LinkedIn's New Hire Learning Paths: A Comprehensive Analysis**
>
> LinkedIn's New Hire Learning Paths represent a strategic approach to employee development and support, emphasising personalised

learning and mentorship from the outset. This programme is designed to integrate new hires into the company while investing in their growth and professional development. Here's an in-depth look at how LinkedIn's New Hire Learning Paths function and the impact they have on new employees.

1. Personalised Learning Paths

The New Hire Learning Paths at LinkedIn are a cornerstone of the company's onboarding process, tailored to meet the specific needs and goals of each new employee:

- **Customised training modules:** New hires are provided with customised training modules that are tailored to their roles, skills and career aspirations. These modules include a mix of online courses, interactive workshops and self-paced learning materials. This personalisation ensures that the training is relevant and aligned with the new hire's job responsibilities and career goals.

Example: LinkedIn Learning Paths for Engineers

For new hires in technical roles, such as software engineers, LinkedIn offers specialised learning paths that include training on their specific technology stack, coding best practices and project management tools. This targeted approach helps new engineers quickly become proficient in the technologies and processes used at LinkedIn.

- **Role-specific content:** The learning paths are designed to include content that is specific to the new hire's role within the company. This includes foundational knowledge necessary for their position, as well as advanced topics that support ongoing professional development.

2. Mentorship Opportunities

Mentorship is a key component of LinkedIn's New Hire Learning Paths, providing new employees with guidance and support as they acclimate to their new roles:

- **Assigned mentors:** Each new hire is paired with an experienced mentor who provides one-on-one support. The mentor helps the new employee navigate their role, understand company culture and address any challenges they may face. This relationship offers valuable insights and personalised advice, enhancing the onboarding experience.

Example: LinkedIn's Mentorship Programme

LinkedIn's mentorship programme pairs new hires with mentors who are not only experts in their fields but also trained to support and guide new employees. These mentors help new hires set goals, provide feedback and offer advice on career development.

- **Regular check-ins:** The mentorship relationship includes regular check-ins to discuss progress, address any concerns and provide ongoing support. These check-ins ensure that new hires have a consistent source of guidance and feedback.

3. *Commitment to Continuous Learning*

LinkedIn's New Hire Learning Paths reflect the company's commitment to continuous learning and professional growth:

- **Ongoing development:** Beyond initial training, LinkedIn encourages new hires to pursue ongoing learning opportunities. This includes access to a wide range of learning resources, such as LinkedIn Learning courses, industry conferences and professional development workshops.

Example: LinkedIn Learning Platform

New hires have access to LinkedIn Learning, an online platform offering thousands of courses on various topics. This platform allows employees to continue their education and stay updated on industry trends, supporting their long-term career development.

- **Career growth opportunities:** The learning paths are designed to align with employees' career goals, helping them develop the skills needed for future advancement within the company. LinkedIn's focus on career growth ensures that employees are prepared for new challenges and opportunities.

4. *Impact on New Hires*

The New Hire Learning Paths at LinkedIn have several positive effects on new employees:

- **Enhanced onboarding experience:** Personalised learning paths and mentorship help new hires integrate into their roles more effectively, leading to a smoother onboarding experience. Employees feel supported and equipped to tackle their responsibilities.
- **Increased engagement:** The emphasis on professional development and growth demonstrates LinkedIn's appreciation for employees' potential, leading to increased engagement and motivation.
- **Skill development:** By providing targeted training and mentorship, LinkedIn helps new hires build the skills necessary for their current roles and future career advancement.

Example: LinkedIn's Employee Satisfaction Ratings

LinkedIn's focus on learning and development contributes to high employee satisfaction ratings. The company's commitment to employee growth and support is reflected in positive feedback from employees who value the opportunities for continuous learning and career development.

5. *Long-Term Benefits*

The benefits of LinkedIn's New Hire Learning Paths extend beyond the initial onboarding period:

- **Career advancement:** The programme helps new hires develop the skills and knowledge needed for career advancement, supporting their long-term growth within the company.

- **Employee retention:** By investing in employees' professional development and demonstrating appreciation for their potential, LinkedIn enhances employee retention and reduces turnover.
- **Cultural integration:** The learning paths and mentorship opportunities reinforce LinkedIn's culture of continuous improvement and support, helping new hires align with the company's values and mission.

Conclusion

LinkedIn's New Hire Learning Paths exemplify how personalised learning and mentorship can significantly enhance the onboarding experience. By providing customised training, pairing new hires with experienced mentors and supporting ongoing development, LinkedIn demonstrates its commitment to employee growth and professional success. This comprehensive approach not only helps new employees integrate smoothly into their roles but also fosters long-term engagement, satisfaction and career advancement.

Creating a Culture of Appreciation

Building a culture of appreciation from day one involves intentional and consistent efforts to make new staff members feel valued. By welcoming them warmly, providing supportive orientation, recognising their early contributions, integrating them into the team and offering continuous development, school leaders can foster an environment where every employee feels appreciated and motivated to contribute their best.

This approach not only enhances individual satisfaction and performance but also strengthens the overall school culture, creating a positive, supportive and productive environment for everyone.

Conclusion

As we come to the close of this chapter, the centrality of appreciation in building a thriving school culture has never been clearer. Through insights from elite sports teams, innovative businesses and successful educational settings, we've seen how authentic recognition can transform an environment, making it a place where staff feel valued, supported and motivated. When appreciation is not just a token gesture but a core part of the school's ethos, it strengthens the bonds between colleagues and uplifts the entire organisation.

Appreciation is not simply about handing out praise – it's about acknowledging the effort, commitment and unique strengths that each staff member brings to the table. From the meticulous janitor who ensures the school is a welcoming space to the administrative staff managing endless schedules, every role matters, and every contribution deserves recognition. As leaders, it is our responsibility to create structures that foster a culture of appreciation, from small everyday acknowledgements to formal systems of recognition.

We've also explored practical strategies, from implementing regular 'shout-outs' and personalised thank-you notes, to celebrating both individual and team achievements. These are not grand gestures, but they are transformative when consistently applied. They provide validation, build trust and foster a sense of belonging, ultimately enhancing staff wellbeing and productivity.

As you reflect on how to apply these ideas within your own school, consider how even small shifts in how you express appreciation could lead to meaningful change. The ripple effects of genuine recognition can be profound, helping to create a work environment where every person feels seen, valued and motivated to do their best.

Reflective Questions

1. **How do you currently recognise and appreciate the contributions of your staff?** Reflect on whether recognition is frequent and genuine. Are all roles within your school equally appreciated, or are some overlooked?
2. **What systems are in place to ensure that appreciation is part of the school culture?** Consider whether you have formal mechanisms like awards or shout-outs, and if these are perceived as meaningful by your staff.
3. **Is appreciation equally spread between individual and team accomplishments?** Reflect on whether there is a balance in recognising individual achievements versus collaborative successes. Does your culture foster healthy teamwork?

4. **What steps can you take to create a more personalised approach to showing appreciation?** Could you implement practices like handwritten notes, one-on-one acknowledgements, or specific feedback that highlights the value of each staff member's contributions?
5. **How does appreciation impact your team's morale and effectiveness?** Think about times when recognition has lifted morale or driven positive results. What can you learn from these moments, and how can you replicate them more frequently?

References and Further Reading

Bock, L. (2015). *Work Rules! Insights from Inside Google That Will Transform How You Live and Lead.* Twelve.

Brailsford, D. (2017). *Mastermind: How Dave Brailsford Reinvented the Wheel.* Yellow Jersey Press.

Chouinard, Y. (2006). *Let My People Go Surfing: The Education of a Reluctant Businessman.* Penguin Books.

Collins, J. (2001). *Good to Great: Why Some Companies Make the Leap… and Others Don't.* HarperBusiness.

Freiberg, K., & Freiberg, J. (2003). *Nuts! Southwest Airlines' Crazy Recipe for Business and Personal Success.* Bard Press.

Gibson, K. (2018). 'United Airlines reconsiders swapping employee bonuses with lottery.' CBS News. www.cbsnews.com/news/united-airlines-bonus-lottery-being-reconsidered-company-says

Graban, M. (2012). *Lean Hospitals: Improving Quality, Patient Safety, and Employee Engagement.* CRC Press.

Hancock, P. (2024). *Employee Recognition Programmes: An Immanent Critique.* Sage Journals.

Humphries, J., & Hughes, D. (2021). *High Performance: Lessons from the Best on Becoming Your Best.* Penguin Life.

Jones, G. R., & George, J. M. (1998). 'The Experience and Evolution of Trust: Implications for Cooperation and Teamwork.' *Academy of Management Review*, 23(3), 531–546.

Jordan, M. (1998). *The Life: Michael Jordan's Story.* Bantam Books.

Lencioni, P. (2002). *The Five Dysfunctions of a Team: A Leadership Fable.* Jossey-Bass.

Paneinto, J. (2015). 'Good Leaders Aren't Afraid to Be Nice.' *Harvard Business Review*. https://hbr.org/2015/04/good-leaders-arent-afraid-to-be-nice

Porath, C., & Pearson, C. (2013). 'The Price of Incivility.' *Harvard Business Review*. https://hbr.org/2013/01/the-price-of-incivility

Smith, J. (2018). *Employee Recognition and Engagement in the Digital Age*. Wiley.

Society for Human Resource Management (SHRM). (2016). *Employee Job Satisfaction and Engagement: Revitalizing a Changing Workforce*. https://wfpma.org/files/research/getabstract-2016-employee-job-satisfaction-and-engagement.pdf

Chapter 7
Growth and Development

In the competitive worlds of business and sport, the principle of continuous growth and development is a non-negotiable factor for success. Companies and teams alike invest heavily in cultivating their talent, recognising that the progress of their people is intrinsically linked to their overall performance. This chapter explores the concept of growth and development in the educational context, drawing parallels from notable practices in business and sport to illustrate how schools can implement similar strategies to support and elevate their staff.

Manchester City's Elite Development Squad

In the realm of sport, the Manchester City Football Club has garnered attention for its comprehensive approach to player development through the Elite Development Squad (EDS). This programme is not just about honing athletic skills but also focuses on the holistic development of young players, including education, personal development and life skills training. The EDS aims to nurture players' talents from an early age, ensuring they are well prepared for the demands of professional football and life beyond the pitch.

Manchester City's commitment to developing well-rounded individuals exemplifies the importance of a supportive environment that fosters growth in all aspects of a person's life. The club's success on the field is often attributed to this thorough approach, which ensures that players not only excel in their sport but also mature as individuals capable of handling the pressures and challenges of professional sports.

The Educational Parallel: Investing in Teacher Growth

Drawing inspiration from these examples, schools can adopt a similar ethos by investing in the growth and development of their staff. Just as Manchester

City has shown, fostering a culture of continuous learning and development leads to greater innovation, job satisfaction and organisational success. In education, this translates to more engaged and effective teachers, which in turn leads to better student outcomes.

To foster an environment that promotes growth and development, school leaders must prioritise ongoing professional development, provide access to resources for personal and professional growth, and create opportunities for staff to take on new challenges and responsibilities. This chapter will delve into practical strategies for achieving these goals, demonstrating how schools can emulate the best practices from business and sport to cultivate a thriving, dynamic educational environment.

Reimagining Growth and Development: Lessons from Business and Sport

As we transition into an era where the pace of change is relentless, the traditional methods of leadership and professional development are being re-evaluated. A significant indicator of this shift is the closure of General Electric's (GE) iconic Crotonville leadership development centre. Once a beacon of corporate training, this facility represented the old guard's belief in centralised, intensive training programmes designed to mould future leaders. GE's decision to sell Crotonville signals a broader shift in how organisations view and implement growth and development strategies. It underscores the need for more agile, personalised and digitally enabled learning solutions, a sentiment echoed by other corporations like 3M and Boeing, who are also moving away from their traditional leadership campuses.

The Shift from Traditional to Agile Leadership Development

Traditionally, companies like GE and IBM built their reputation on robust, centralised training programmes. These programmes focused on broad leadership principles and long-term courses, aiming to create well-rounded managers capable of leading diverse business units. However, as the business landscape evolved, these methods began to show their limitations. The needs of businesses became more specific and rapidly changing, demanding a shift from generalised training to more tailored, adaptive learning experiences.

Insights from the Digital Revolution in Learning at Microsoft

Microsoft exemplifies the shift from traditional to agile learning with its integration of digital platforms and personalised learning paths. Recognising that different roles require different skills, Microsoft leverages its vast resources to provide targeted training and development opportunities. This includes their Microsoft Learn platform, which offers role-based learning paths, certifications and interactive learning modules accessible anytime, anywhere. By embracing a digital-first approach, Microsoft ensures that its employees can continually develop skills that align with the company's strategic goals and the evolving needs of the technology sector.

Sporting Example: The Evolution of Player Development in the NBA

In the sports world, the NBA's approach to player development has also evolved to become more personalised and data-driven. Teams now use advanced analytics and technology to tailor training regimens to the specific needs of individual players. The Toronto Raptors, for instance, have been at the forefront of using data analytics to enhance player performance and development. By monitoring players' physiological data and tailoring training sessions accordingly, the Raptors ensure that each player receives the specific support they need to excel, whether it's improving their shooting accuracy or increasing their stamina (Bo G, 2018; Mina, 2024).

Implementing Growth and Development in Schools: A Blueprint for Success

Drawing lessons from these examples, schools can revitalise their approach to staff growth and development by implementing a few key strategies.

1. *Identify Core Capabilities: Tailoring Development to Organisational Needs*

To implement an effective growth and development programme, schools must first identify the specific skills and capabilities that are most critical to their success. This involves analysing the characteristics of highly successful educators and leaders within the organisation to determine what sets them apart. Schools should then tailor professional development programmes to cultivate these key capabilities in other staff members.

For instance, if a school's top educators share a common strength in innovative curriculum design or strong classroom management, these areas should be emphasised in training programmes. This targeted approach ensures that development efforts are directly aligned with the school's strategic goals and the unique challenges it faces.

2. *Develop a Robust Measurement Strategy: Evaluating Impact and Effectiveness*

Measuring the impact of growth and development programmes is crucial to their success. Schools should establish a comprehensive measurement strategy that includes both quantitative and qualitative data. This could involve pre- and post-training assessments, surveys, focus groups and performance metrics.

For example, the implementation of new teaching techniques learned during professional development could be evaluated through student performance data, classroom observations and teacher self-assessments. The goal is to create a feedback loop that not only measures the efficacy of the programme but also provides ongoing insights that can be used to refine and improve future training.

3. *Embrace a Hybrid Learning Model: Blending Digital and In-Person Learning*

A hybrid approach that combines digital learning platforms with in-person or virtual events can provide a flexible and effective way to deliver professional development. Digital platforms offer the advantage of on-demand, self-paced learning, which is particularly useful for busy educators. These platforms can include a range of resources such as video tutorials, interactive modules and discussion forums.

However, to maximise the impact of these resources, it's important to incorporate interactive and social elements. In-person or virtual workshops, seminars and peer-to-peer learning sessions allow for deeper engagement and the opportunity to discuss and apply new knowledge in a collaborative setting. Schools can further enhance these experiences by incorporating elements of gamification, such as earning badges or completing challenges, to motivate and engage participants.

4. Leverage External Expertise: Bringing in Fresh Perspectives and Best Practices

While internal development resources are invaluable, collaborating with external experts can provide fresh perspectives and access to cutting-edge best practices. Schools can partner with educational consultants, industry experts or organisations specialising in professional development to create customised programmes that address specific needs. These partnerships can help introduce new methodologies and insights that may not be available within the school.

For example, schools might work with a technology company to develop training programmes on the latest digital tools and teaching strategies. These collaborations can be particularly beneficial in areas where the school may lack internal expertise, ensuring that staff have access to the most current and effective practices.

So what does this look like in schools?

Professional Development Plans: Crafting Personalised Learning Journeys

To truly empower educators, schools should work with teachers to create individualised professional development plans that align with their career goals and interests. These plans serve as roadmaps, guiding teachers on their journey of growth and helping them focus on areas that they are passionate about or wish to improve.

1. Funding and Resources for Professional Growth

A key aspect of these plans involves providing funding or resources for training, workshops and conferences. This investment demonstrates the school's commitment to its teachers' professional growth and helps keep them abreast of the latest educational trends and methodologies. For instance, a teacher interested in integrating technology into the classroom could attend a tech-focused education conference, while another might pursue a workshop on differentiated instruction.

2. Collaborative Goal-Setting

The process of developing professional development plans should be collaborative, involving discussions between teachers and school leaders. This ensures that the plans are not only aligned with individual aspirations but also support the broader goals of the school. Regular check-ins and updates to these plans can help track progress and adjust goals as needed, fostering a continuous loop of feedback and improvement.

Moving Beyond Traditional Appraisals: The Teacher Development Plan

Traditional teacher appraisals, often characterised by formal lesson observations and copious documentation, have long been a source of stress and contention. Many educators find these evaluations unhelpful, as they often focus on criticism rather than constructive support. To create a more supportive and growth-oriented environment, schools can shift towards a teacher development plan (TDP) that emphasises peer coaching and ongoing professional support.

1. Scrapping Formal Lesson Observations

Under the TDP model, formal lesson observations are replaced with informal visits focused on support rather than judgement. This approach fosters a culture of openness and continuous improvement, as teachers feel more comfortable experimenting with new teaching strategies without the fear of punitive assessments. These visits are opportunities for constructive feedback and collaboration, not critique.

2. Emphasising Peer Coaching

Peer coaching is a central component of the TDP, allowing teachers to learn from each other's strengths and experiences. Experienced teachers can share effective practices with their peers, while newer teachers can offer fresh perspectives. This reciprocal relationship not only enhances teaching skills but also builds a stronger sense of community within the school.

3. Streamlining the Appraisal Process

By keeping the appraisal programme brief and focused, schools can minimise the administrative burden on teachers and reduce stress. Documentation should be concise and meaningful, capturing essential feedback and goals without being overly cumbersome. The emphasis should be on actionable insights that genuinely help teachers improve their practice.

Mentorship Programmes: Building Supportive Relationships

Establishing mentorship programmes is a powerful way to support professional growth and foster a sense of belonging and community among teachers. Pairing experienced educators with newer ones provides a valuable support network, allowing new teachers to navigate the challenges of the profession with guidance and encouragement.

1. Structured Mentorship Initiatives

A structured mentorship programme should include clear objectives and expectations for both mentors and mentees. Mentors can provide practical advice on classroom management, curriculum development and school policies, while also offering emotional support. Regular meetings and check-ins ensure that the relationship is productive and that mentees are receiving the guidance they need.

2. Benefits Beyond Professional Growth

Mentorship programmes not only enhance professional skills but also contribute to a positive school culture. They help new teachers feel welcomed and valued, reducing feelings of isolation and burnout. Moreover, mentors themselves often find the experience rewarding, as it allows them to reflect on and refine their own practices while giving back to the teaching community.

Creating a Sense of Community: Fostering Belonging Among Staff

A strong sense of community is vital for staff wellbeing. Just as schools focus on creating a supportive environment for students, it is equally important to cultivate a culture where staff feel connected and valued.

1. Engaging Staff in School Activities

Schools can engage staff in a variety of activities that promote team spirit and camaraderie. For example, incorporating staff into the school's house system – if one exists – can be an excellent way to build a sense of belonging. Organising competitions, quizzes and social events specifically for staff can create opportunities for bonding outside of the classroom setting.

2. Celebrating Milestones and Achievements

Recognising and celebrating the achievements and milestones of staff members is another powerful way to build community. This could include acknowledging anniversaries, professional milestones or personal accomplishments in staff meetings or newsletters. Such recognition not only boosts morale but also fosters a culture of mutual respect and appreciation.

Career Pathways: Facilitating Professional Growth and Leadership

Creating clear and accessible pathways for career advancement within the school is essential for retaining motivated and ambitious teachers. Schools should offer opportunities for staff to take on leadership roles and explore new areas of interest.

1. Leadership Opportunities

Schools can provide a range of leadership roles, from department heads to curriculum developers. Encouraging teachers to pursue these roles allows them to develop new skills and take on greater responsibilities, enriching their professional experience. It also benefits the school by cultivating a pipeline of skilled leaders ready to take on key positions.

2. Supporting Continuing Education

Support for continuing education, such as advanced degrees or certifications, is another important aspect of career development. Schools can offer financial assistance or time off for staff pursuing further education, demonstrating their commitment to the long-term professional growth of their teachers.

Differentiating Support: Tailoring Development to Individual Needs

Recognising that teachers are at different stages in their careers, it's important for schools to provide differentiated support that meets the unique needs of each staff member.

1. Early Career Teachers

Early career teachers may benefit from practical support, such as funding for classroom supplies or access to teaching resources. They may also need more frequent mentorship and professional development opportunities focused on foundational teaching skills.

2. Mid-Career and Senior Teachers

For mid-career and senior teachers, development opportunities might include leadership training, time for research or curriculum development, or sabbaticals to pursue advanced studies. Providing tailored support ensures that all staff members continue to grow and feel valued, regardless of their career stage.

Strengths-Based Approach: Focusing on What Works

As we discussed in an earlier chapter, a strengths-based approach shifts the focus from deficits to strengths, encouraging schools to build on what they do well and leverage those strengths to address challenges. This is where we can really utilise and bring this strengths-based approach to life.

1. Celebrating Strengths

Schools should regularly highlight and celebrate the strengths and successes of their staff. This positive focus helps build a constructive and motivated work environment. Whether it's exceptional teaching practices, innovative projects or strong community engagement, recognising these strengths fosters a culture of excellence and positivity.

2. Leveraging Strengths for Improvement

By identifying and utilising the strengths of staff members, schools can more effectively address areas for improvement. For instance, teachers who excel in technology can lead training sessions to help their colleagues integrate digital tools into their classrooms. This not only utilises existing expertise but also promotes a collaborative culture where everyone contributes to the school's success.

Fostering a culture of growth and development is essential for the well-being and professional satisfaction of school staff. By implementing personalised professional development plans, embracing supportive appraisal practices, establishing mentorship programmes, creating a strong sense of community, offering clear career pathways, providing differentiated support and adopting a strengths-based approach, schools can create an environment where teachers thrive. Drawing inspiration from successful practices in business and sport, these strategies not only enhance the individual capabilities of educators but also contribute to the overall success and innovation within the educational institution.

The Risks and Challenges of Mismanaging Growth and Development in Schools

While the benefits of well-executed growth and development programmes in schools are clear, the potential pitfalls of mismanagement can have significant negative repercussions. Recognising these risks and challenges is essential for school leaders and educators to mitigate them effectively.

Risks of Poorly Designed Professional Development Programmes

- **Lack of relevance and engagement:** One of the most significant risks in professional development is the design and implementation of programmes that are not aligned with teachers' needs or interests. When training sessions are generic or irrelevant, or fail to consider the specific context of the school, they can lead to disengagement and frustration among teachers. This disengagement not only wastes resources but can also demotivate staff, reducing the overall effectiveness of teaching and learning.
- **Inadequate support and resources:** Even well-intentioned development initiatives can falter if they are not adequately supported by sufficient resources – whether financial, material or human. For example, if a school introduces a new technology without providing adequate training and technical support, teachers may struggle to integrate it into their classrooms effectively. This lack of support can lead to stress and burnout, negatively affecting both teacher wellbeing and student outcomes.
- **Overemphasis on appraisal over development:** A common challenge is balancing the need for accountability with the need for genuine professional growth. When appraisals are too rigid, overly focused on metrics or punitive, they can create a culture of fear rather than one of learning. Teachers may focus on meeting the bare minimum requirements rather than taking risks and innovating in their practice. This environment stifles creativity and can lead to a superficial compliance rather than meaningful improvement.

Challenges in Implementation

- **Cultural resistance:** Changing established practices and mindsets is inherently challenging. In schools with long-standing traditions or entrenched cultures, introducing new professional development initiatives can be met with resistance. This resistance can stem from a fear of change, lack of trust in leadership or previous negative experiences with professional development. Addressing these cultural barriers requires thoughtful communication, inclusive planning processes and consistent, transparent leadership.

- **Balancing time and priorities:** Teachers often face significant time constraints, balancing teaching responsibilities with administrative tasks and personal commitments. Introducing new professional development initiatives can add to their workload, leading to stress and burnout if not carefully managed. Schools must find ways to integrate professional development into teachers' schedules without overwhelming them, such as through blended learning approaches or designated professional development days.
- **Sustainability and continuity:** Ensuring the sustainability and continuity of professional development programmes is another major challenge. Initiatives may lose momentum if they are not continually supported or if key staff members leave the school. Schools need to build robust systems and structures that can withstand changes in personnel and leadership to maintain a consistent focus on professional growth.

Threats and Opportunities

- Threats:
  - **Budget constraints:** Limited funding can severely restrict the scope and quality of professional development initiatives. This can result in under-resourced programmes that fail to meet teachers' needs or deliver meaningful outcomes.
  - **Inequitable access:** Without careful planning, there is a risk that some staff members may have greater access to professional development opportunities than others, leading to disparities in skills and knowledge within the school.
- Opportunities:
  - **Leveraging technology:** The growing availability of online learning platforms offers a significant opportunity to provide flexible, cost-effective professional development. Schools can use these platforms to offer personalised learning paths, access to a wide range of resources and opportunities for collaboration beyond geographical constraints.
  - **Building a collaborative culture:** By focusing on creating a collaborative culture, schools can transform professional development from a top-down mandate into a shared, community-driven initiative. Encouraging peer-to-peer learning and mentorship can not only enhance professional growth but also build a stronger, more supportive school community.

Real-Life Example: Wells Fargo's Sales Culture and Professional Development Issues

A well-known real-life example of mismanaged growth and development in the corporate sector is the Wells Fargo sales scandal. This case illustrates how inadequate professional development and an overly aggressive corporate culture can lead to unethical behaviour and significant reputational damage.

The Wells Fargo Case: Background

Wells Fargo, one of the largest banks in the United States, became embroiled in a massive scandal that emerged publicly in 2016. The bank's employees were found to have opened millions of unauthorised accounts for customers without their knowledge. This unethical practice was driven by an aggressive sales culture that prioritised meeting unrealistic sales targets over ethical behaviour and customer service.

Key Issues in Professional Development and Management

- **Unrealistic sales targets:** Wells Fargo set exceedingly high sales targets for its employees, which were tied directly to their performance evaluations and incentives. The pressure to meet these targets was immense, leading employees to engage in unethical practices, such as opening accounts without customer consent. This focus on sales metrics over professional and ethical development contributed significantly to the scandal.
- **Inadequate training and support:** Employees were not adequately trained on ethical sales practices or how to manage the pressure of the sales targets. The lack of proper training and support created an environment where employees felt compelled to meet targets by any means necessary, including illegal and unethical actions.
- **Poor leadership and cultural oversight:** The leadership at Wells Fargo failed to establish a culture of accountability and integrity. Reports indicated that some managers were aware of the unethical

practices but did little to stop them. The absence of strong ethical guidance and oversight allowed these practices to become widespread.
- **Lack of ethical development focus:** The professional development programmes at Wells Fargo lacked a focus on ethics and customer service. Instead, the programmes emphasised sales techniques and metrics. This oversight contributed to a culture where the end justified the means, and ethical considerations were sidelined.

Consequences

The fallout from this scandal was severe. Wells Fargo faced significant fines and legal action, and the scandal led to the resignation of several high-level executives, including the CEO. The company's reputation suffered greatly, and it lost customer trust, which impacted its business operations and stock value.

Lessons Learned

The Wells Fargo scandal serves as a cautionary tale for organisations about the dangers of prioritising metrics and sales over ethical standards and proper professional development. It highlights the importance of creating a balanced development strategy that includes not only skills and performance metrics but also ethical considerations and customer-centric values.

In conclusion, the Wells Fargo case underscores the necessity of a comprehensive approach to professional development that integrates ethical training, realistic goal-setting and strong leadership oversight. This balanced approach helps prevent the kind of widespread unethical behaviour that can lead to significant corporate crises.

Summary

Navigating the complexities of professional development in schools requires a balanced approach that acknowledges potential pitfalls and actively works to mitigate them. By recognising the risks, such as lack

> of relevance, insufficient resources and cultural resistance, schools can proactively address these challenges. At the same time, leveraging the opportunities provided by technology and a collaborative culture can help schools to create a robust professional development framework that supports all staff members. Ultimately, the goal is to foster an environment where professional growth is continuous, inclusive and impactful, leading to better outcomes for both teachers and students.

The Essential Role of Professional Development in Educational Improvement

Research consistently underscores the critical role of professional development in enhancing educational outcomes. As Borko (2004) and others have noted, continuous professional learning is crucial for transforming classroom practices, improving school environments and ultimately bettering student learning outcomes. Professional development should be deeply embedded in the daily life of the school, characterised by ongoing, contextualised and collaborative learning opportunities. This aligns with the findings of Timperley (2011) and Little (2012), who emphasise the importance of workplace learning environments that facilitate dynamic and interactive exchanges among teachers.

The Shift from Traditional to Collaborative Learning Models

Traditional professional development often occurs in isolated, workshop-style settings that, while useful, are limited in their impact. Instead, contemporary research advocates for a more integrated approach where professional learning is job-embedded and contextualised. This means that learning occurs in real time, within the specific context of the teachers' work, making it more relevant and immediately applicable. As Fullan (2007) suggests, professional learning that is deeply embedded in teachers' specific subject areas and aligned with the school's overall development goals is most effective in bringing about real changes in classroom practices.

The Importance of School Leadership and Culture

The role of school leadership in fostering a culture of continuous learning cannot be overstated. Leaders are instrumental in creating an environment that supports teacher development by identifying individual and collective development needs, encouraging experimentation and allocating resources for learning. Thoonen et al. (2011) and Vanblaere and Devos (2016) highlight the need for leaders to actively promote a positive learning culture that aligns structures, values and relationships within the school.

Walker (2007) emphasises that a thriving teacher learning culture depends on the alignment of these components, with leaders ensuring that the conditions for effective learning are in place. This includes fostering a sense of professional trust, autonomy and providing the necessary time and resources. Such an environment not only supports individual teacher growth but also facilitates collective learning and improvement across the school.

Collaborative Models and Their Impact

Collaborative models of professional development, such as lesson study (LS), are gaining traction for their ability to bring about sustained changes in teaching practices. The LS model involves teachers collaboratively planning, observing and analysing lessons, fostering a shared responsibility for student learning and professional growth. This model is supported by research from Vangrieken et al. (2015), which found that teacher collaboration leads to higher job satisfaction, increased innovation in teaching and stronger self-efficacy beliefs.

However, it is important to note that while collaborative practices are beneficial, they are not a panacea. The changes they bring about can be subtle and incremental rather than dramatic. This highlights the importance of having outside experts, such as local scientists or university faculty, to challenge teachers' preconceived notions and expand their horizons of observations (Ermeling & Yarbo, 2016). Such external inputs can provide fresh perspectives and help teachers to envision new possibilities for their classroom practices.

The Role of Teacher Leadership in Professional Development

Teachers themselves can play a pivotal role in driving professional development within their schools. Teacher leadership, as explored by Alexandrou and Swaffield (2014), involves teachers taking on leadership roles to facilitate broader professional development initiatives. The principles outlined by MacBeath and Dempster (2008) for effective teacher leadership include focusing on the learning of all members of the school community, creating conducive conditions for learning and maintaining accountability.

For teacher leadership to flourish, certain conditions must be met, including professional trust, perceived autonomy, supportive administrators and the availability of time and resources. Schools that foster such conditions not only enhance individual teacher growth but also contribute to a culture of continuous improvement and innovation.

The Future of Professional Development in Schools

The evolving landscape of professional development calls for a more holistic, integrated and collaborative approach. As schools navigate the complexities of modern education, they must move beyond traditional methods and embrace practices that are responsive to the unique needs of their teachers and students. This includes leveraging technology for digital learning, creating flexible and differentiated support systems, and fostering a culture that celebrates strengths and encourages continuous improvement.

By adopting these strategies, schools can not only improve individual teacher performance but also drive systemic school-wide improvements. The goal is to create learning environments where teachers feel valued, supported and empowered to take risks and innovate. As research has shown, when teachers thrive, so do their students, leading to better educational outcomes and a more vibrant school community.

Final Thoughts

The journey of professional development is ongoing and dynamic, requiring a commitment from all stakeholders – teachers, school leaders and the broader educational community. By embracing a comprehensive approach that includes personalised learning plans, supportive peer coaching, collaborative models and strong leadership, schools can create a culture of continuous growth and development. This culture not only benefits teachers but also has a profound impact on students and the entire school community. As we look to the future, it is clear that the most successful schools will be those that prioritise the professional development of their staff, recognising that this is the key to unlocking the full potential of every student.

Conclusion

As we conclude this chapter on fostering growth and development within school environments, it's clear that a holistic approach to professional development can be transformative, not only for individual staff members but also for the school community as a whole. Growth and development are continuous processes, driven by intentional investment, support and encouragement from leadership. Just as professional sports teams and leading businesses have found, the most substantial successes come from empowering individuals to reach their full potential. In the same way, schools that prioritise staff development create a nurturing environment where educators feel valued, engaged and inspired to make meaningful impacts in their classrooms and beyond.

Schools that commit to a culture of growth and development see ripple effects throughout their entire communities. Educators equipped with the right skills and support can better adapt to the evolving demands of their profession, enrich their teaching practices and inspire their students. By building this foundation of support, schools can create a legacy of excellence and resilience that endures beyond any one programme or initiative.

Reflective Questions

1. What strategies do we already use to encourage and support staff development in our school? How effective have these been?
2. How can we create more personalised development plans that align with both the goals of our staff and the wider mission of our school?
3. Are there areas where our development initiatives might benefit from integrating elements of peer coaching, mentorship or external expertise?

4. How can we measure the impact of our professional development programmes to ensure they're meeting both individual and organisational goals?
5. What changes might we implement to ensure our approach to staff development remains flexible, inclusive and responsive to the needs of our educators?

References and Further Reading

Alexandrou, A., & Swaffield, S. (2014). 'Teacher Leadership: A Review of Research.' *Educational Management Administration & Leadership, 42*(3), 352–369.

Bo G. (2018). 'Toronto Raptors: Machine Learning as a Method for Improving the Roster Decision Process.' Harvard Business School Digital Initiative. https://d3.harvard.edu/platform-rctom/submission/toronto-raptors-machine-learning-as-a-method-for-improving-the-roster-decision-process

Borko, H. (2004). 'Professional Development and Teacher Learning: Mapping the Terrain.' *Educational Researcher, 33*(8), 3–15.

Ermeling, B. A., & Yarbo, R. (2016). 'Teacher Learning through Lesson Study: The Role of Outside Experts.' *Teaching and Teacher Education, 56*, 80–89.

Fullan, M. (2007). *The New Meaning of Educational Change* (4th ed.). Teachers College Press.

Garrison, D. R., & Vaughan, N. D. (2020). *Blended Learning in Higher Education: Frameworks and Approaches*. San Francisco: Jossey-Bass.

Hargreaves, A., & Fullan, M. (2019). 'The Power of Professional Capital: A Model for School Leadership and Teacher Development.' *International Journal of Leadership in Education, 22*(5), 456–473.

Joyce, B., & Showers, B. (2022). 'Student Achievement through Peer Coaching: A Guide for Teachers.' *Educational Leadership, 78*(3), 24–31.

Little, J. W. (2012). 'Teachers' Professional Development in a Climate of Educational Reform.' *Educational Policy, 46*(5), 795–812.

Livingstone, D., & Flynn, R. (2024). 'Rethinking Leader Development: Lessons from the Closure of General Electric's Crotonville.' McChrystal Group. www.mcchrystalgroup.com/insights/detail/2024/05/03/rethinking-leader-development--lessons-from-the-closure-of-general-electric-s-crotonville

MacBeath, J., & Dempster, N. (2008). *Connecting Leadership and Learning: Principles for Practice*. Routledge.

Manchester City Football Club. (2024). 'Elite Development Squad (EDS).' www.mancity.com/news/eds-academy/2024-review-manchester-city-elite-development-squad-63870977

Mina, A. C. (2024). 'The numbers don't lie: Raptors' statistical excellence explained.' Raptors Rupture. https://raptorsrapture.com/the-numbers-dont-lie-raptors-statistical-excellence-explained-nba-advanced-stats-analytics

Thoonen, E. E. J., Sleegers, P. J. C., Oort, F. J., & Peetsma, T. T. D. (2011). 'How to Improve Teaching and Learning in Schools: A Study of the Factors That Promote Professional Learning.' *Educational Administration Quarterly, 47*(4), 597–619.

Timperley, H. (2011). 'The Role of Educational Leaders in Professional Learning and Development.' *Journal of Educational Leadership, 68*(5), 63–77.

Vanblaere, B., & Devos, G. (2016). 'The Role of School Leadership in the Development of a Learning Organization.' *Journal of Educational Administration, 54*(5), 574–589.

Vangrieken, K., Dochy, F., Raes, E., & Kyndt, E. (2015). 'Teacher Collaboration: A Systematic Review.' *Educational Psychologist, 50*(3), 220–243.

Walker, A. (2007). 'School Leadership in an Era of Change: Challenges and Strategies.' *Educational Leadership, 65*(3), 22–27.

Chapter 8
Empathy

Empathy is not just a soft skill – it is a leadership imperative. Consider the approach of New Zealand's Prime Minister, Jacinda Ardern, during the COVID-19 pandemic. Her empathetic leadership became a global example, as she consistently communicated with care, recognising the real human toll of the crisis. Ardern's daily briefings weren't just about data and restrictions; they were filled with messages of compassion and solidarity. She listened to the concerns of her citizens, validated their fears and made decisions with their wellbeing at the forefront. In schools, leaders must adopt a similar mindset.

For school leaders, empathy begins with understanding the pressures and emotions staff experience every day. From the newly qualified teacher struggling to find their feet to the long-in-the-tooth teacher facing burnout, each member of staff has unique challenges. A leader's ability to listen, show understanding and act accordingly can transform the culture of a school. Empathy allows leaders to see beyond the immediate needs of the institution and focus on the individuals that make it run, creating a school environment where staff feel supported, valued and understood. This chapter will explore how empathy not only fosters a supportive environment but also enhances staff wellbeing and performance.

Empathy in Action: Satya Nadella at Microsoft

A powerful example of empathetic leadership from the business world is Satya Nadella, the CEO of Microsoft. Since taking the helm in 2014, Nadella has been credited with not only revitalising Microsoft but also transforming its corporate culture. Nadella's leadership style is rooted in empathy – a trait he developed through personal experiences, including raising a child with special needs. He has spoken openly about how this shaped his perspective on leadership, teaching him to lead with compassion and understanding. Nadella's empathetic approach helped to create an environment where innovation and collaboration thrive.

Nadella emphasises that empathy is a key source of business innovation, as he discussed in his interview with Wharton's Adam Grant in 2018. He stated that while empathy is often regarded as a 'soft skill', it is essential for grasping customers' unmet needs and understanding the experiences of employees. Nadella had to learn to cultivate this empathy, especially after the birth of his son Sain, who has cerebral palsy. He candidly shared how this personal experience helped him realise that the focus needed to be on his son's needs, not on his own challenges. In a similar way in a school, poor leaders often focus on the challenges they face, rather than removing barriers to their staff's wellbeing. This journey towards greater empathy has driven many of Microsoft's initiatives, including tools aimed at improving accessibility for those with disabilities.

Under Nadella's leadership, Microsoft has thrived because he brought empathy into decision-making processes and company culture. He understands that leaders need to listen to the unique needs of their teams and their customers, and he has consistently emphasised the importance of building a culture where learning, collaboration and empathy are prioritised. This lesson translates well to education, where school leaders must also be attuned to the diverse needs of their staff and students, making decisions with their wellbeing in mind.

Empathy and Resilience: Paul Polman at Unilever

Another exemplary leader who has harnessed the power of empathy is Paul Polman, the former CEO of Unilever. Polman's tenure was marked by his commitment to sustainability and his belief that businesses should act with a greater sense of purpose beyond profits. But what truly set Polman apart was his empathetic approach to leadership. He believed that empathy was essential not only in understanding customers but in caring for employees, encouraging them to contribute to a shared vision of social and environmental responsibility.

Polman's empathetic leadership style fostered resilience within Unilever's workforce. By prioritising employee wellbeing and ensuring that staff felt connected to the company's higher purpose, he created a culture where employees were more motivated, engaged and productive. He frequently listened to his employees' concerns and made decisions that reflected their input, reinforcing a sense of shared ownership and community within the company.

In schools, leaders can mirror this by connecting staff wellbeing with a broader vision of purpose. When teachers feel that their personal wellbeing is valued alongside the success of their students, they are more likely to feel motivated and resilient, even in the face of challenges. For example, a leader could ensure that wellbeing days or mental health initiatives are not seen as isolated events but part of a broader commitment to creating a nurturing and inclusive environment for both staff and students. Just as Polman created a sense of purpose at Unilever, school leaders can inspire staff by aligning wellbeing initiatives with the school's mission and values.

Empathy in Education: Deborah Meier and Small School Leadership

Deborah Meier, a pioneering educator and advocate for the small schools movement in the United States, offers another powerful example of empathetic leadership in education. Meier's approach to leadership was rooted in the belief that relationships are the foundation of effective education. She emphasised the importance of small, close-knit school communities where teachers, students and families all knew each other well. This intimate setting allowed teachers to feel more connected to their colleagues, their students and the wider school community, fostering a culture of mutual support and understanding.

Meier's schools were designed with empathy at their core. She recognised that for teachers to be effective, they needed to feel heard and valued. Teachers in her schools had significant autonomy over curriculum and were encouraged to collaborate with their peers to create a learning environment that met the unique needs of their students. By fostering trust and empowering teachers, Meier demonstrated how empathy could transform a school community.

School leaders today can take a page from Meier's book by ensuring that staff feel empowered to make decisions that affect their work and their students. Some of the schools today are huge institutions approaching 2,000 students and 250 staff. Creating smaller, collaborative teams within larger schools can mimic the tight-knit community of Meier's small schools, providing teachers with the support network they need to thrive. Empathy, in this case, means recognising that teachers are not just employees but key stakeholders in the school's success and giving them the voice and agency to shape that success.

Empathy and Compassion: A Delicate Balance

While empathy is crucial for effective leadership, it's also important to balance it with compassion. As Rasmus Hougaard, Jacqueline Carter and Marissa Afton highlight in their article, 'Connect with Empathy, But Lead with Compassion' (2021), leaders have been thrust into roles where they are not only expected to lead but also support their teams emotionally. For almost two years, leaders have had to bear the emotional weight of their staff's struggles, which can be overwhelming. Their article emphasises the need for leaders to understand the distinction between empathy and compassion.

Compassion involves understanding what another person is feeling and having the willingness to act to alleviate their suffering. While empathy allows leaders to connect deeply with their staff, it can also lead to emotional exhaustion if leaders find themselves continually absorbing the feelings of others. This realisation is crucial for school leaders, who must navigate the emotional landscape of their staff's experiences without becoming overwhelmed themselves.

Paul Polman (2019) articulates this balance well when he states, 'If I led with empathy, I would never be able to make a single decision.' His insight illustrates that while empathy helps leaders connect with their teams, it can cloud judgement. Leaders must be able to take a step back, understand their own emotional responses and lead with compassion to make effective decisions that benefit everyone.

Avoiding the Empathy Trap – and Leading with Compassion

Overcoming an empathetic hijack is a critical skill for any leader. In mastering this skill, leaders must remember that being wary of overdoing empathy does not make them less human or less kind. Rather, it makes them better able to support people during difficult times. Strategies for leading with compassion include:

1. Taking a Mental and Emotional Step Away

Creating emotional distance is a crucial strategy for leaders facing challenging situations. When emotions run high, it can be easy for leaders to become overwhelmed by the feelings of those they are supporting, which may cloud their judgement and decision-making capabilities. By taking a mental step back, leaders can gain a clearer perspective on the situation at hand. This distance allows them to assess the challenges objectively, identify the underlying issues and develop actionable solutions without being hindered by emotional responses. Emotional detachment does not imply a lack of empathy; rather, it enables leaders to remain calm and focused, ensuring that they can effectively support their team without sacrificing their own mental health.

2. Asking What They Need

One of the most effective ways for leaders to demonstrate support is by simply asking their staff, 'What do you need?' This question is powerful in its simplicity, as it opens the door for honest dialogue and allows employees to express their concerns, needs and preferences. By actively soliciting input from their team, leaders can gain valuable insights into how best to support each individual. This practice not only validates employees' feelings but also fosters a culture of collaboration and trust. When staff feel heard and valued, they are more likely to engage openly with leadership, which can lead to more tailored support and solutions that genuinely meet their needs.

3. Remembering the Power of Non-Action

In a fast-paced environment, leaders often feel compelled to offer solutions or take immediate action to address problems. However, there are times when the most effective form of support is simply to listen. Remembering the power of non-action can be transformative for both leaders and their teams. When leaders provide their presence and willingness to listen, it allows individuals to express their thoughts and emotions freely, creating a safe space for reflection. Sometimes people need to articulate their experiences without being interrupted by problem-solving efforts. By embracing this approach, leaders can offer immense support that fosters trust and emotional healing, allowing team members to process their feelings and arrive at their own conclusions.

4. Coaching the Person to Find Their Own Solution

Rather than jumping in to solve problems for their staff, effective leaders focus on coaching individuals to find their own solutions. This approach encourages employees to take ownership of their challenges and fosters resilience. By guiding team members through a process of reflection and self-discovery, leaders can help them develop critical thinking skills and confidence in their decision-making abilities. Coaching creates an environment where staff feel empowered and capable, rather than reliant on others to fix their problems. This method also strengthens the relationship between leaders and their team, as it promotes mutual respect and collaboration, ultimately contributing to a more positive and productive workplace culture.

5. Practising Self-Care

Leaders often face significant emotional labour as they support their teams through challenges. To sustain their ability to lead effectively, it is essential for them to prioritise their own wellbeing through self-care practices. This involves recognising the mental and emotional toll that leadership can take and actively seeking strategies to recharge and maintain resilience. Whether through setting boundaries, engaging in regular physical activity or taking time for hobbies and relaxation, leaders must cultivate their own health to model positive behaviours for their staff. When leaders demonstrate the importance of self-care, it not only enhances their effectiveness but also encourages a culture where staff members feel empowered to prioritise their wellbeing, creating a more balanced and supportive environment for everyone.

Think of how powerful it is when leaders leave on time. How, when they walk out, they talk about how they are going to the pub, pick up their kids, go to the gym. Now think of the reverse, when leaders don't leave on time and make judgements about those who do. When they leave but talk about all the work they have to do. Practising self-care is one of the most powerful management tools a leader can leverage.

Empathy, therefore, is an essential quality for effective leadership, particularly in challenging times. However, balancing empathy with compassion allows leaders to make sound decisions while supporting their staff effectively. As school leaders take cues from the empathetic approaches of Ardern, Nadella, Polman, and Meier, they will be better equipped to foster a culture of wellbeing that empowers and uplifts their teams, ultimately enhancing the educational experience for both staff and students.

Prioritising Mental Health: Practical Support for Staff

While empathy forms the foundation of a supportive school culture, it must be paired with tangible mental health resources to ensure staff feel valued and supported. Effective school leadership involves proactively creating structures that help staff manage their mental health, reducing stress and improving overall wellbeing.

One crucial resource is access to professional counselling services. Schools should consider partnerships with independent bodies, such as Westfield Health or employee assistance programmes (EAPs), which offer confidential, accessible counselling to staff members. These services provide a safe space where educators can discuss personal or professional concerns with trained professionals outside of the school environment. Leaders who make such services available send a clear message: staff wellbeing matters, and support is always there when needed.

In addition to professional services, fostering a culture of peer support can enhance wellbeing within the school community. Introducing staff wellbeing ambassadors – volunteers trained to support colleagues in managing stress, workload or personal challenges – can make a significant difference. These ambassadors serve as a first point of contact for staff who may feel overwhelmed but aren't ready to seek formal counselling. They help create an environment where people look out for one another, building trust and solidarity within the team. Having designated ambassadors also signals that mental health is a priority embedded into the fabric of the school's culture.

Finally, supportive line management is essential for sustaining staff wellbeing. Leaders should ensure that line managers are not just responsible for overseeing performance but also for regularly checking in on the wellbeing of their team. This involves creating a structure where managers have both the time and the training to conduct meaningful conversations about workload, stress and work–life balance. Regular one-on-one meetings, where staff are encouraged to speak openly about their pressures, are an important tool in identifying issues early and offering support before stress becomes overwhelming. Leaders should provide managers with the skills to listen empathetically, ask the right questions and signpost staff to further support where necessary.

Implementing Staff Wellbeing Ambassadors: A Practical Guide

Introducing staff wellbeing ambassadors into your school can significantly enhance the support network available to staff. The success of this initiative hinges on careful planning and training, with a focus on creating a culture where wellbeing is prioritised, stigma is broken and staff feel empowered to seek help. Here's a step-by-step guide on how to put these ambassadors in place effectively:

1. Encourage Volunteering and Build a Critical Mass

The first step is to open the role of wellbeing ambassadors to volunteers. Volunteering ensures that those taking on the role are passionate about staff wellbeing and are motivated by a genuine desire to help their colleagues. Aim for a wide range of volunteers across different departments, roles and levels of experience. This ensures that every staff member has someone they can relate to, whether they are a teaching assistant, administrative staff or senior teacher.

Having a diverse group of ambassadors allows for better coverage, both in terms of reaching all areas of the school and offering varied perspectives. Encourage volunteers who may have lived experiences of mental health challenges to come forward, as they can offer insight and empathy grounded in personal experience. Building a critical mass of ambassadors ensures that the workload is shared and that support is available when needed.

2. Provide Comprehensive Training

Once you've identified volunteers, the next crucial step is providing them with the training necessary to make a positive impact. This training should focus on three key areas.

a. **Information-Sharing: Breaking the Stigma Around Mental Health**

One of the core roles of wellbeing ambassadors is to break the stigma surrounding mental health within the school environment. They need to be equipped with up-to-date information about mental health issues and the available resources, so they can share this knowledge confidently. Training should focus on building an understanding of common mental health concerns such as anxiety, depression and stress. Ambassadors should be able to share this information with colleagues in an accessible and non-judgemental way, making mental health discussions a normal part of staffroom conversations.

Encouraging openness about mental health helps create a culture where it's okay to talk about challenges. Ambassadors should lead by example, openly discussing wellbeing initiatives, mental health resources and their role in supporting staff, whether through informal chats or during staff meetings.

b. Practical Skills: Active Listening and Supporting Key Areas

Empathy and active listening are at the heart of a wellbeing ambassador's role. Training should equip ambassadors with the practical skills to listen without judgement, offer appropriate emotional support and know when to escalate concerns. These skills are particularly important in sensitive areas such as bereavement, work-related stress and personal difficulties.

Workshops on active listening will help ambassadors become more attuned to colleagues who may be struggling but reluctant to voice their concerns. Role-playing scenarios on how to handle difficult conversations, knowing the limits of their role and signposting staff to professional help are all essential components of their training. This ensures that ambassadors are confident and capable in their role, knowing when they can assist and when to refer to further support.

c. Feedback Loop: Continual Improvement and Support

Finally, it's crucial to create a feedback mechanism that allows ambassadors to share their experiences and suggestions for improving the programme. Ambassadors should feel supported in their roles and not left to handle everything alone. Schedule regular check-ins with ambassadors where they can discuss any challenges they face, share success stories and offer ideas for further training or resources. These meetings also allow leadership to monitor the effectiveness of the initiative and adjust it as needed.

Creating a continual feedback loop ensures that the wellbeing ambassador programme evolves to meet the changing needs of the school. By seeking feedback from both ambassadors and the staff they support, you can keep the initiative fresh and responsive, ensuring it remains a vital part of the school's wellbeing strategy.

Insights From Barclays' Mental Health Awareness Group

In the corporate world, Barclays provides a strong example of how staff wellbeing ambassadors or groups can foster a supportive culture. A significant initiative is the Mental Health Awareness Group, which was founded in New York by Peter Toal, a senior executive in Barclays' Investment Bank. Peter, who had personally faced challenges with depression and anxiety, recognised the need to create a more empathetic and open environment in the high-pressure finance industry.

The group, part of the Reach Disability and Mental Health Network, focuses on breaking the stigma around mental health by encouraging employees to share their personal stories, organising awareness events and providing practical resources like meditation sessions and stress management workshops. Through these efforts, they've cultivated a culture where employees are more comfortable discussing their mental wellbeing, thus normalising mental health conversations in the workplace.

This initiative also offers key lessons that can be applied in schools:

- **Volunteering and leadership**: The group was started by Peter after he identified a gap in mental health support in his office. Similarly, in schools, encouraging staff to volunteer to become wellbeing ambassadors can ensure that those who are passionate about mental health take the lead.
- **Training and awareness**: Barclays focused on training staff to recognise mental health issues, share their experiences and engage in open discussions. Schools can adopt this model, ensuring that wellbeing ambassadors are trained to provide both emotional and practical support while helping to break the stigma surrounding mental health.
- **Inclusive support systems**: The Mental Health Awareness Group also integrates regular feedback, peer support and meditation practices to improve wellbeing. Schools can replicate these strategies by offering wellbeing sessions, encouraging open conversations and regularly reviewing how staff are supported.

The success of Barclays' programme, which now reaches hundreds of employees, shows that a dedicated group of ambassadors can create a ripple effect, normalising mental health discussions and leading to a more supportive and empathetic environment. In schools, a similar approach can not only enhance staff wellbeing but also promote a healthier, more collaborative workplace culture.

Flexible Work Arrangements: Enhancing Wellbeing Through Flexibility

One of the most impactful ways to support staff wellbeing is by offering flexible work arrangements. In a school environment, flexibility acknowledges that teachers and staff have demanding schedules and often juggle numerous responsibilities, both personal and professional. Implementing adaptable working practices not only boosts morale but also increases productivity and job satisfaction.

1. Taking PPA from Home

Providing the option for teachers to take their planning, preparation and assessment (PPA) time from home is a simple yet effective way to promote work–life balance. Allowing staff to complete this non-contact time remotely gives them the flexibility to work in a comfortable, personalised environment without the constant interruptions that can occur in school. This can help reduce stress levels, enabling teachers to better focus on planning lessons and assessing students' progress with clearer minds.

By trusting staff to manage their time effectively, schools also empower them to feel more in control of their workload. For many, the flexibility to step away from the school environment, even for a few hours, can lead to a significant reduction in stress and increase in wellbeing. Additionally, this practice demonstrates that the school values the autonomy and professionalism of its staff.

Implementing the Off-Site PPA Policy

The off-site PPA policy provides staff with the flexibility to complete their PPA time away from school, supporting wellbeing while ensuring teaching quality is upheld.

- **Purpose and Benefits:** This policy allows staff to take their PPA time off-site, promoting a healthier work–life balance and reducing stress by providing an environment conducive to focus. It enhances teaching quality by offering teachers uninterrupted time for planning and preparation, ultimately leading to better student outcomes.
- **Establish Clear Protocols:** To ensure the policy operates smoothly and fairly, clear protocols are essential:
  - **Approval process:** Off-site PPA must be agreed with the staff member's line manager before each occurrence. This ensures that staffing needs and school responsibilities are met.
  - **Restrictions:** Off-site PPA cannot be taken during important school events such as open evenings or parents' evenings. Staff must also prioritise responsibilities like mentor time.
  - **Attendance tracking:** Staff must sign out when leaving the premises and sign back in upon returning, maintaining accountability and meeting safeguarding requirements.
- **Maintain professionalism and accountability:** While taking PPA off-site, staff are expected to use the time for its intended purpose – planning, preparation and assessment. This means maintaining the same level of professionalism as they would on-site and ensuring that teaching responsibilities are upheld without disruption to student outcomes.
  - **Focused planning:** Teachers should use off-site PPA to work on deep, uninterrupted planning to enhance the quality of lessons and teaching resources.
- **Foster collaboration with line managers:** To ensure consistency and fairness, decisions regarding off-site PPA should be at the discretion of line managers, who will consider the impact on both the department and overall school operations.
  - **Criteria for approval:** Line managers should assess each request based on school-wide activities, staffing levels and the staff member's role and responsibilities.
  - **Transparent communication:** Ensure clear communication between staff and line managers about the expectations and boundaries for off-site PPA.
- **Regular monitoring and evaluation:** To assess the impact of the off-site PPA policy, regular reviews are necessary. The policy should be evaluated based on its effect on both staff wellbeing and student outcomes.

- **Feedback mechanism**: Gather input from staff and line managers to make adjustments and ensure that the policy remains fair, consistent and effective.

2. The One-Hour Cover Card

Another practical way to support staff wellbeing is through the introduction of a one-hour cover card. This card would allow staff to take up to an hour off at any point in the school year, without needing to justify the time. Whether it's for a medical appointment, a personal errand or simply to rest and recharge, the one-hour cover card can make a huge difference in staff feeling supported.

This policy signals a trust-based approach to staff management. Teachers and staff are often bound by rigid schedules, but a flexible option like this provides a small but important reprieve when unexpected needs arise. It can also foster a culture of understanding, where the mental and emotional needs of staff are respected as part of their overall wellbeing.

Implementing the Cover Card Policy

Introducing a cover card policy is a practical way to support staff wellbeing by providing flexibility for teachers to manage occasional personal or professional commitments. Drawing on the example from Penistone Grammar School, here's a structured approach to successfully implementing this policy in your school:

- **Purpose and benefits:** The cover card policy offers staff the opportunity to request cover for one lesson or one hour per academic year. This enables teachers to handle unexpected situations without using their PPA time or feeling overburdened by their workload. It promotes work–life balance and reduces stress, while ensuring continuity of student learning through a structured cover process.
- **Establish Clear Protocols:** For the policy to work effectively, it is crucial to develop and communicate clear guidelines:
    - **Eligibility:** Each staff member is entitled to use the cover card for one lesson/hour per academic year.

- **Approval process:** Staff must request cover through a formal system, which is then reviewed by their line manager. Requests should be made at least 48 hours in advance to allow time for arranging cover.
- **Restrictions:** Cover cannot be requested during critical school events (e.g. inspections, open evenings), and line managers have discretion to approve or deny requests based on school operational needs.
- **Minimise disruption to learning:** While the policy prioritises staff wellbeing, it's essential to ensure that student learning remains unaffected:
  - **Lesson planning:** Teachers using the cover card must provide detailed lesson plans and materials to the covering teacher to maintain consistency in teaching quality.
  - **Balanced use:** Keep accurate records of cover card usage to ensure equitable distribution and prevent overuse.
- **Foster professional accountability:** Even when using the cover card, teachers should take responsibility for the smooth running of their classes. This involves maintaining transparency with their line managers and ensuring that all necessary preparations are in place before taking time off.
- **Regular policy review:** Finally, ensure that the policy is regularly assessed to track its impact on staff wellbeing and teaching quality. Seek feedback from staff and line managers to identify any areas for improvement and make adjustments as needed to align with the school's evolving needs.

Implementation and Communication

For these initiatives to succeed, it is essential that they are communicated clearly to all staff. Leaders should ensure that teachers and other staff members are aware of their right to take PPA from home and use their one-hour cover card as needed. Regularly promoting these policies through staff briefings, email reminders and team meetings helps create an atmosphere where flexibility is embraced as part of the school's ethos.

Wellness Programmes for Staff Wellbeing

Implementing wellness programmes in schools can have a transformative impact on staff wellbeing by addressing both their physical and mental health needs. Offering a holistic approach to staff care not only improves morale but can also have positive knock-on effects on teaching quality, staff retention and student outcomes. Schools should consider tailoring wellness initiatives based on staff feedback to ensure these programmes meet their unique needs.

1. Focus on Mental and Physical Wellbeing

To support the mental and physical health of staff, wellness programmes should encompass a range of offerings, such as:

- **Workshops on stress management:** Stress is one of the leading factors in burnout. Regular workshops focused on managing stress can provide staff with practical tools to navigate challenging situations. These could include time management strategies, relaxation techniques and emotional resilience training.
- **Mindfulness and self-care techniques:** Mindfulness sessions or self-care workshops can help staff refocus, manage anxiety and build a more positive working mindset. Practices like meditation or simple breathing exercises could be incorporated into the school day, offering moments of reflection and calm.
- **Physical health programmes:** Encouraging physical activity, such as offering free gym memberships or organising group fitness sessions, can significantly enhance staff wellbeing. Flu jabs or other preventive health measures are small but effective ways of showing the school's commitment to staff health.

2. Tailor Programmes to Staff Needs

It's essential that wellness programmes reflect what staff truly want and need. Engaging staff in decision-making will create buy-in and make the programmes more successful. A simple survey or feedback loop can help identify preferences and priorities.

For example:

- Some staff might prefer physical health initiatives, such as discounted gym memberships or exercise classes.

- Others might prioritise mental health workshops on resilience, stress management or even access to counselling services.
- Schools could also offer free flu jabs, a low-cost initiative that helps reduce sickness during the academic year, which is especially valuable in environments where absences can have significant operational impacts.

3. The Impact of Wellness Programmes

Although wellness initiatives may require investment, the returns in terms of staff productivity, job satisfaction and reduced absenteeism can be substantial. Healthier, more engaged staff are better equipped to meet the demands of teaching and contribute positively to school culture.

In addition, wellness programmes are a powerful tool for retaining experienced staff, who might otherwise leave due to burnout or overwhelming stress. The positive psychological impact of knowing their school values their wellbeing cannot be understated.

4. Building a Sustainable Wellness Culture

Wellness programmes should not be one-off initiatives but part of a long-term strategy to build a sustainable culture of wellbeing. Schools should regularly review the success of their wellness offerings through staff feedback, adjust them as necessary and consistently promote participation.

 ## Insights from Salesforce's Ohana Culture

Salesforce, a global leader in customer relationship management (CRM) software, has not only transformed the tech industry with its innovative products but also cultivated a unique corporate culture known as the Ohana culture. This approach emphasises family, trust and community, significantly contributing to high employee satisfaction in a competitive industry.

Origins and Development

Founded in 1999 by Marc Benioff, Salesforce rapidly ascended to prominence in the tech landscape, offering cloud-based solutions to businesses worldwide. As the company expanded, it faced challenges in maintaining employee satisfaction and fostering a positive work environment amidst increasing competition. To tackle these issues, Salesforce introduced the Ohana culture, drawing inspiration from the Hawaiian concept of family. This cultural framework seeks to create an inclusive and supportive environment where employees feel valued and connected.

Key Components of Ohana Culture

- **Employee wellbeing:** The Ohana culture prioritises the mental and physical wellbeing of its employees. Salesforce offers various wellness programmes, including mental health support, fitness reimbursements and flexible work policies, promoting a healthy work–life balance.
- **Community and trust:** The culture fosters a sense of belonging and trust among employees. Initiatives like volunteering opportunities allow staff to engage with their communities, reinforcing the notion that they are part of something larger than themselves.
- **Professional development:** Salesforce encourages continuous learning and growth, offering resources for professional development and opportunities for career advancement. This investment in employees helps them feel supported in their professional journeys.
- **Collaboration and support:** Ohana culture emphasises teamwork and collaboration. Employees are encouraged to share ideas, support one another, and work together towards common goals, enhancing overall productivity and morale.

Impact and Lessons Learned

The implementation of Salesforce's Ohana culture has yielded significant positive outcomes, including improved employee satisfaction, increased retention rates and enhanced overall business success. By fostering a strong, inclusive corporate culture, Salesforce demonstrates how prioritising employee wellbeing can lead to a more engaged and productive workforce.

Conclusion

Empathy is more than an attribute of effective leadership; it's the foundation upon which thriving, resilient and supportive school communities are built.

When leaders embrace empathy, they foster environments where staff feel valued and understood, enabling them to bring their best selves to their work each day. As we've seen through the examples of leaders like Jacinda Ardern, Satya Nadella and Paul Polman, empathy is a powerful force for positive change, uniting people around shared goals and creating workplaces where everyone is empowered to succeed.

For schools, empathetic leadership isn't just about feeling what others feel – it's about making intentional choices that prioritise staff wellbeing, actively listening to concerns and providing meaningful support. By creating a culture of empathy, schools can bridge the gap between policy and practice, enabling staff to flourish both personally and professionally.

Reflective Questions

1. How can we integrate empathy into our daily interactions with staff to strengthen our school community?
2. What tangible steps can we take to ensure that our wellbeing initiatives reflect a commitment to empathy?
3. How might we balance empathy with compassion, ensuring that we lead with understanding while still making decisions that benefit the whole community?
4. In what ways can we better empower our staff to voice their needs and challenges openly, knowing that they'll be met with understanding and support?
5. How can our school leadership model empathetic practices that encourage staff to prioritise their wellbeing and, in turn, contribute to a positive school culture?

References and Further Reading

Allen, T. D., & Eby, L. T. (2007). 'The Relationship Between Work-Family Balance and Employee Well-Being: A Review and Research Agenda.' *Journal of Vocational Behavior*, 70(2), 169–181.

Ardern, J. (2020). 'COVID-19: A Message of Solidarity and Compassion from Prime Minister Jacinda Ardern.' New Zealand Government. www.beehive.govt.nz/speech/pm-address-covid-19-update

Barclays. (n.d.). 'Cultivating a wellbeing culture.' https://labs.uk.barclays/learning-and-insights/team-and-culture/wellbeing/cultivating-a-wellbeing-culture

Benioff, M. (2019). *Trailblazer: The Power of Business as the Greatest Platform for Change*. Penguin Press.

Grant, A. (2018). *Interview with Satya Nadella on Empathy and Leadership*. Wharton School of the University of Pennsylvania. Retrieved from www.wharton.upenn.edu

Hougaard, R., Carter, J., & Afton, M. (2021). 'Connect with Empathy, but Lead with Compassion.' *Harvard Business Review*. https://hbr.org/2021/12/connect-with-empathy-but-lead-with-compassion

Meier, D. (1995). *The Power of Small Schools: The Case for a New Educational Environment*. The New Press.

Nadella, S. (2018). 'Empathy as a Key Source of Innovation at Microsoft.' In A. Grant (Ed.), *The Empathy Factor: Leading with Care* (pp. 135–145). Wharton School Publishing.

National Education Association. (2020). 'Creating a Culture of Wellness in Schools: Supporting Staff and Students.' www.nea.org/student-success/great-public-schools/student-educator-mental-health

Polman, P. (2019). 'Sustainable Leadership at Unilever: Prioritizing People, Planet, and Profit.' Unilever. Retrieved from www.unilever.com

Salesforce. (n.d.). 'Salesforce Ohana and Hawaiian Culture: Embracing Community.' www.salesforce.com/blog/salesforce-and-hawaii

Conclusion

As we reach the conclusion of this book, it's vital to reiterate why change in staff wellbeing is not just necessary, but urgent. The state of teacher wellbeing in the UK has reached a breaking point, and it's an issue that is far more than a fleeting concern; it's a crisis that, if left unresolved, will lead to long-term damage not just to individual schools but to the entire educational system. Across the country, educators are grappling with stress, burnout and feelings of being undervalued. We cannot continue to treat this as a background issue or something to be addressed in isolated initiatives. This isn't a case of adding a wellbeing day to the school calendar or putting up posters reminding staff to take breaks. It is about rethinking how we treat the profession of teaching itself.

In schools today, many teachers face immense pressure, not only from the growing demands of the job but from a system that often fails to provide them with the necessary emotional, logistical or even physical support. The workload keeps increasing – marking, lesson planning, tracking data, managing behavioural challenges – yet the resources available to teachers seem to diminish year by year. Worse still, the pandemic has amplified these problems. Remote teaching, ever-changing guidelines and a shift to hybrid models of education have tested the resilience of teachers in ways that were unimaginable just a few years ago. If we truly believe in the transformative power of education, then we must prioritise the wellbeing of those on the frontlines of delivering it: our teachers. They are the foundation of the system. If that foundation cracks or collapses, the entire structure falls with it.

It is no longer enough to see teacher wellbeing as a 'nice-to-have' addition to school life. It must become an essential, non-negotiable aspect of how schools operate. Change is no longer optional – it is imperative. The demands placed on teachers have evolved, yet the structures in place to support them have stagnated. The profession has moved forward in terms of technological advances, pedagogical approaches and curriculum changes, but the support systems – whether through mentoring, workload management or emotional support – have remained stubbornly outdated. Teachers are asked to do more with less, and as we have seen, many are choosing to leave the profession entirely as a result. Those who remain are often battling burnout and exhaustion, barely keeping their heads above water.

What exacerbates this situation is the disconnect between leadership and teaching staff in many schools. Leaders, particularly those who have not been in the classroom recently, can sometimes be out of touch with the daily realities faced by their teachers. They may not understand the full extent of the pressure teachers are under, or they may simply underestimate the toll that these pressures take on mental and physical health. This disconnect leads to decision-making that can feel arbitrary or even punitive, further alienating staff who already feel unsupported. We find ourselves in a system where teachers are expected to manage increasing workloads, navigate a complex web of administrative tasks and, in many cases, take on roles that stretch far beyond their initial job description. And while we ask more of them, we provide fewer resources to support their mental and emotional health. This imbalance is unsustainable.

Teacher wellbeing cannot be an afterthought in policy discussions or school strategies. It needs to be brought to the forefront, and the conversations around it need to shift from being reactive to proactive. Too often, schools only address wellbeing after a crisis has occurred – when a teacher has had to take extended sick leave due to stress or when staff morale has hit rock bottom. This is too late. The time to intervene is long before these crises develop, and the approach must be systemic, continuous and embedded into the very fabric of school life. Wellbeing must be seen not just as a way to 'keep teachers happy' but as a critical factor in creating a successful, thriving school. The wellbeing of our teachers is intrinsically linked to the success of our students.

Research consistently shows that teachers who feel supported and valued are not only more likely to remain in the profession, but they also create more positive and effective learning environments for their students. A teacher's mental state is directly tied to their ability to engage with students, manage classrooms effectively and deliver high-quality teaching. When a teacher feels valued and supported, they bring that positive energy into the classroom. The reverse is also true: a teacher who is overworked, undervalued and stressed can struggle to manage the demands of the job, which can have a direct impact on student outcomes. Therefore, the connection between teacher wellbeing and student success cannot be overstated.

This is why school leadership has such a pivotal role to play. As schools face staffing shortages and retention crises, the need to build and maintain a strong, resilient workforce is greater than ever. Yet, for too long, the focus has been on metrics, standards and test scores, while the wellbeing of the people at the heart of the school system has been overlooked. The obsession with measurable outcomes has often come at the expense of the very people expected to deliver those outcomes. Leaders must begin to ask themselves: How can we expect teachers to give their best to students when they themselves are running on empty? How can we improve student performance if the very people who are tasked with making that happen are struggling under the weight of unbearable pressure?

It's important to recognise that no policy, no framework and no system will work if the people implementing it are burnt out. Schools that ignore the wellbeing of their staff will find themselves facing not only higher turnover rates but also lower engagement, increased absenteeism and declining student performance. In contrast, schools that prioritise staff wellbeing will not only see an improvement in teacher retention but also in student engagement, attendance and academic achievement. We cannot ignore this anymore. Wellbeing has to move from being a peripheral concern to being at the centre of all school strategy and planning.

What we need now is a cultural shift. This is not about making small adjustments or introducing short-term fixes. It is about changing the way we think about leadership, management and the role of teachers within our schools. School leaders must make wellbeing a core pillar of their leadership strategy, not an afterthought. It requires brave decisions, a willingness to rethink outdated practices and, above all, an understanding that the wellbeing of staff is not a 'nice-to-have' – it is a necessity. When we fail to prioritise staff wellbeing, we are failing our teachers, our students and, ultimately, the future of education. We need to reimagine how schools are run so that staff wellbeing is seen as essential as curriculum design or exam preparation.

To do this, leaders need to be bold. They need to be willing to question long-standing practices and routines that may no longer serve the needs of their staff. For instance, we need to rethink how we structure school days, how we allocate workloads and how we handle teacher evaluations. We need to ask ourselves if the systems we have in place are helping or hindering the wellbeing of our staff. Change will not happen overnight, and it will require effort, but the schools that embrace this change will not only see their staff thrive but also witness the ripple effect on student outcomes, community engagement and overall school success.

A key part of this cultural shift is the understanding that wellbeing is not just about reducing workloads or offering mental health resources – although those are important. It's about creating a work environment where teachers feel valued, respected and empowered. This means giving teachers a voice in decision-making, providing opportunities for professional growth, and fostering a supportive school community where staff are encouraged to collaborate and support one another. It's about creating a culture of appreciation, where the contributions of teachers are recognised and celebrated, and where their personal and professional needs are considered in every aspect of school life.

We have spent too long tinkering at the edges. Small initiatives, while well meaning, are not enough. We need to overhaul how we approach staff wellbeing and make it a foundational element of our school cultures. This is not about offering quick fixes or one-off wellbeing days; it is about building lasting, systemic change that places staff wellbeing at the heart of every decision, every policy, every interaction. It's about integrating wellbeing into the very DNA of how schools operate, so that it is no longer something that is considered 'extra' but something that is fundamental to the success of the school.

The CAGE framework, which we have explored throughout this book, offers us a structured roadmap for achieving this. Communication, Appreciation, Growth and Development, and Empathy and Support are not just theoretical concepts – they are the building blocks of a school culture where staff wellbeing is prioritised. Each element of the CAGE framework plays a vital role in creating an environment where teachers can thrive. However, it is not enough to simply implement these practices in isolation. They need to be part of a coherent, integrated approach that permeates every aspect of school life.

The CAGE framework provides us with the tools to move from intent to action. But the real power of this framework lies in its flexibility and adaptability. Every school is different – different demographics, different challenges, different strengths. The beauty of the CAGE model is that it can be tailored to fit the unique needs of each school, and it gives leaders the flexibility to prioritise wellbeing without feeling constrained by a rigid set of rules. It is a framework, not a formula, which means it requires thoughtful implementation and reflection.

Communication is the first pillar of the framework for a reason. Without open, transparent communication, any wellbeing initiative is doomed to fail. Teachers need to know that they can voice their concerns without fear of reprisal and that their input will be taken seriously. Too often, communication in schools is one-way, with leadership passing down decisions that teachers are expected to follow without question. This top-down approach can alienate staff and foster a culture of resentment. Instead, schools must prioritise two-way communication, where staff feel comfortable sharing their ideas, concerns and feedback. This not only builds trust but also helps leaders make more informed decisions that genuinely address the needs of their staff.

We must also rethink how we hold staff meetings. In many schools, these meetings are lengthy, dominated by announcements and information-sharing that could easily be communicated via email or bulletin. Instead of using this precious time to talk at staff, schools should create spaces for dialogue and collaboration. Informal feedback sessions, such as coffee mornings or drop-in forums, can be more effective in gathering staff insights and fostering a sense of community. It is also crucial to implement systems where staff can provide anonymous feedback. People are more likely to be honest about their concerns when they don't fear repercussions, and anonymous feedback mechanisms give staff the opportunity to raise issues that they may otherwise keep to themselves.

Moreover, the calendar plays a significant role in communication. A poorly planned calendar can make life unnecessarily difficult for teachers. Consider this: if parent evenings are scheduled on back-to-back days, or open evenings fall during particularly busy times of the year, the workload for teachers can become unbearable. Yet, with a few small adjustments – such as spacing out events or ensuring that busy evenings are followed by lighter days – the stress can be significantly reduced. This requires school leaders to be thoughtful in their planning and, crucially, to involve teachers in the process. Leaders should engage middle leaders and staff when setting the calendar, using their feedback to create a schedule that works for everyone.

The second pillar, **Appreciation**, might seem like a simple concept, but its impact on staff wellbeing cannot be overstated. People thrive when they feel valued. Unfortunately, in many schools, recognition of staff contributions can be inconsistent or non-existent. Teachers work long hours, often putting in extra effort outside of the classroom, and yet their hard work often goes unnoticed. A culture of appreciation is not about grand gestures; it's about small, consistent acknowledgements of the value that each teacher brings to the school. Whether it's a handwritten note from a member of leadership, a public acknowledgement during a staff meeting or an email recognising a job well done, these moments of appreciation contribute significantly to job satisfaction and overall wellbeing.

One innovative approach to appreciation is implementing a peer recognition system. Encouraging teachers to acknowledge each other's efforts builds a sense of camaraderie and mutual respect. Programmes like 'Secret Angel' or similar initiatives allow staff to anonymously recognise their colleagues' contributions, spreading positivity throughout the school. Appreciation should also be built into the professional development process. Instead of focusing solely on areas for improvement during appraisals, leaders should highlight each teacher's strengths and contributions, fostering an environment where staff feel empowered and motivated to continue excelling.

A critical aspect of appreciation, which is often overlooked, is the allocation of duties outside the classroom. In many schools, teachers who excel in their classroom roles are often burdened with extra duties – whether it's bus duty, after-school clubs or managing difficult parent interactions. While these tasks are part of school life, overburdening teachers with such responsibilities can undermine the appreciation of their core work. Where possible, leadership should step in and take on these additional tasks, allowing teachers to focus on what they do best – teaching. This sends a clear message: 'We value what you do in the classroom, and we want to give you the space to continue doing it effectively.'

The third pillar, **Growth and Development**, is crucial for fostering long-term teacher satisfaction. Teachers, like all professionals, need opportunities for personal and professional growth. Yet, in too many schools, professional development is either treated as a tick-box exercise or is disconnected from the individual needs and aspirations of staff. A one-size-fits-all approach to professional development is not only ineffective but also demotivating. Schools must create individualised professional development plans for each teacher, aligning training opportunities with their career goals and interests. This may include providing funding for external courses, offering mentorship programmes or simply creating space for teachers to explore new teaching methods and strategies within their own classrooms.

Additionally, it's important to differentiate between teacher development and appraisal. In many schools, formal lesson observations are used as a tool for appraisal, but this often creates a culture of judgement rather than support. Instead, schools should focus on a teacher development plan that emphasises peer coaching and collaboration. By creating a culture of continuous learning – where teachers feel comfortable inviting their colleagues into their classrooms for feedback and support – schools can foster an environment where professional growth is celebrated, not feared. A strengths-based approach to development also allows teachers to build on what they do well, rather than focusing solely on areas for improvement. When teachers feel that their growth is supported and celebrated, they are more likely to engage with professional development opportunities and bring fresh ideas into their classrooms.

Mentorship programmes are another critical element of growth and development. New teachers, particularly early career teachers, often feel overwhelmed by the demands of the profession. Mentorship provides them with the guidance and support they need to navigate these challenges. Experienced teachers can offer advice, share strategies and provide emotional support, helping to build confidence and competence in their less experienced colleagues. But mentorship should not be limited to new teachers. Mid-career and experienced teachers also benefit from having a mentor who can help them explore leadership opportunities, transition into new roles or simply offer a sounding board for new ideas. Creating a culture of mentorship not only supports individual growth but also fosters a sense of community and collaboration within the school.

The final pillar, **Empathy and Support**, is perhaps the most foundational, and the one I want us to really dive deep into to end this book. Empathy is the glue that holds all the other pillars together. It is what allows leaders to understand the needs of their staff, to recognise when someone is struggling and to respond with compassion. Schools are complex, demanding environments, and it is easy for teachers to feel isolated or overwhelmed. A school culture built on empathy ensures that staff feel heard, understood and supported. Leaders must model this empathy in their interactions with staff, creating an environment where teachers feel comfortable sharing their concerns without fear of judgement. Without this, all the other pillars don't work.

Supporting staff goes beyond offering a sympathetic ear – it means putting in place the practical supports that allow teachers to thrive. Mental health resources should be readily available to all staff, whether through access to counselling services, employee assistance programmes or simply by promoting a culture where it's okay to ask for help. Schools should actively work to reduce the stigma around mental health and encourage staff to prioritise their own wellbeing. This could include offering wellness programmes focused on stress management, mindfulness or self-care techniques. It's also important to be flexible with work arrangements. Teachers, like anyone, have personal responsibilities that may occasionally require flexibility. Offering staff the option to work from home when appropriate or allowing for flexible hours can make a significant difference to their mental wellbeing.

Peer support networks are another vital tool for fostering a culture of empathy and support. These networks provide teachers with a safe space to share their experiences, offer advice, and provide emotional support to one another. Encouraging teachers to form these networks can help to build a sense of community and reduce feelings of isolation, particularly in larger schools where staff may not have regular contact with all their colleagues. Schools should actively promote and facilitate these networks, whether through informal meetups, structured support groups or online forums.

As we delve deeper into the need for **Empathy and Support**, it's vital to understand that these aren't just abstract concepts; they are tangible practices that leaders must implement daily. Empathy begins with active listening. It's not enough for leaders to say their doors are always open if they are not genuinely present in conversations with staff. Leaders must be attentive, asking probing questions to understand the underlying issues their staff may be facing. Empathy is about stepping into the shoes of your teachers – not just understanding their struggles but validating their feelings and showing a commitment to support them. When teachers feel that their leaders truly care, they are far more likely to open up about their challenges and engage in solutions collaboratively.

One practical example of empathetic leadership is adjusting workloads to meet the varying needs of staff. Teachers go through different phases in their careers, and their personal circumstances change over time. A teacher returning from maternity leave may have different needs from an experienced teacher approaching retirement. Empathy means recognising these differences and offering tailored solutions that allow each teacher to do their best work without feeling overwhelmed. Flexible work arrangements, phased returns or lighter teaching loads during particularly stressful periods are all ways to show empathy through action. Schools must normalise these accommodations rather than treating them as exceptional cases.

Another essential aspect of **Empathy and Support** is recognising when it is necessary to step in and offer practical help, particularly in crisis situations. A teacher dealing with a personal tragedy or a particularly challenging class may need more than just kind words – they may need help managing their workload or navigating complex situations. In these cases, school leaders must be prepared to act. Whether it's providing additional support in the classroom, reallocating duties or offering extra time off, empathetic leadership means proactively identifying where help is needed and providing it without being asked.

But empathy doesn't stop with school leadership; it should permeate the entire staff culture. Teachers need to be encouraged to support one another, building a sense of camaraderie and shared responsibility. Peer support networks are a powerful tool in fostering this culture. When teachers have a structured way to share their challenges and successes with colleagues, it strengthens the bonds within the team. These networks can be as simple as buddy systems, where teachers check in with each other regularly, or more formalised groups that meet to discuss specific issues, such as managing difficult behaviour or juggling work–life balance. By promoting a sense of community, schools can ensure that teachers feel supported not only by leadership but by their peers as well.

Empathy also plays a critical role in dealing with mental health challenges. Teaching is a high-stress profession, and the mental health of staff cannot be ignored. Schools must actively create environments where mental health is a priority, offering resources that help staff manage stress, anxiety and burnout. One way to do this is through partnerships with external mental health services, such as counselling or therapy, which staff can access confidentially. Promoting these services and making sure staff know how to access them is key. Schools should also regularly check in with staff through surveys or one-on-one meetings to assess how people are doing mentally and emotionally, identifying potential issues before they escalate.

Another aspect of this is offering wellness programmes tailored to the needs of the staff. These programmes can take many forms – some schools have implemented mindfulness workshops, yoga sessions or meditation classes, while others offer discounted gym memberships or flu jabs. Importantly, schools should ask their staff what would benefit them most, rather than implementing generic wellness initiatives that may not resonate with their specific needs. The goal of these programmes should be to provide tangible benefits that help staff manage their health, both physically and mentally, reducing stress and promoting overall wellbeing.

Schools should also consider implementing flexible work arrangements as a form of support. Flexibility in working hours, the option to work from home occasionally or even phased returns to work after extended absences can have a profound impact on staff wellbeing. For instance, allowing teachers to work from home on non-teaching days to plan lessons or mark work can give them the time and space they need to focus without the distractions and pressures of being physically present in the school building. This flexibility signals to staff that their personal needs are acknowledged and that their wellbeing is a priority, not an afterthought.

However, it's important to strike a balance between flexibility and structure. While flexible work arrangements can provide much-needed relief for staff, schools must also establish clear protocols around these arrangements to ensure fairness and consistency. For example, if certain staff are allowed to take PPA time off-site, there must be transparent guidelines for how this is managed. If not handled correctly, it can lead to feelings of resentment or perceptions of favouritism among staff who don't have the same opportunities. Schools need to communicate clearly about who is eligible for these flexible arrangements, how they can request them and what expectations are attached.

This is where protocols intersect with empathy and flexibility. Flexibility should be embraced, but it must also be balanced with equity and consistency. Teachers need to feel that they are treated fairly and that opportunities for flexible working are available to everyone who needs them, not just a select few. Leaders must be transparent about how these decisions are made and ensure that protocols are applied consistently across the board.

The importance of consistency is also evident in how schools manage appraisals and professional development. In some schools, the appraisal process can feel punitive rather than supportive, with teachers being judged on narrow metrics that don't capture the full scope of their work. This approach not only damages morale but also undermines the potential for growth. Instead, appraisals should focus on development, not just accountability. Leaders should use appraisals as an opportunity to recognise teachers' achievements, discuss areas for growth and offer meaningful support that helps them improve. Appraisals should feel like a conversation, not a checklist, and they should be part of a broader culture of continuous development.

Professional development itself must also be reimagined. Too often, professional development in schools consists of generic, one-size-fits-all training sessions that don't meet the specific needs of individual teachers. This can leave staff feeling disengaged and unmotivated, seeing professional development as just another obligation rather than a genuine opportunity for growth.

Schools must shift away from this model and focus on personalised professional development that aligns with each teacher's strengths, interests and career goals. This could involve offering teachers the chance to attend external courses, providing mentorship opportunities or creating space for teachers to pursue their own projects and interests within the school.

Mentorship is a particularly powerful form of professional development that should be offered at every stage of a teacher's career, not just in the early years. Experienced teachers can benefit just as much from mentorship as new teachers, whether they are looking to take on leadership roles or simply refine their practice. Schools should create structured mentorship programmes that pair teachers with colleagues who can support their growth, offering guidance, feedback and encouragement. These relationships not only help teachers develop their skills but also foster a sense of community and shared responsibility within the school.

Furthermore, schools should take a strengths-based approach to development, focusing on what teachers do well rather than solely on areas for improvement. This approach helps to build confidence and encourages teachers to use their strengths to drive improvements in other areas. Instead of fixating on deficits, schools should celebrate what is working well and look for ways to replicate that success across the school. Leaders should be asking, 'How can we build on our successes?' rather than, 'What's wrong, and how do we fix it?'

A strengths-based approach also allows schools to create a more positive and uplifting environment, where staff feel energised by their successes rather than weighed down by their shortcomings. This mindset shift can have a profound impact on staff wellbeing, creating a culture of optimism and innovation. It also encourages teachers to support one another, sharing their strengths and learning from each other's successes. When schools focus on strengths, they build a culture of collaboration rather than competition, where everyone is working towards the shared goal of creating the best possible learning environment for students.

Lastly, self-care cannot be overstated in its importance to the overall success of a wellbeing initiative. Leaders often neglect their own wellbeing in the rush to meet the demands of their roles, but self-care is critical not just for their own health but for setting an example for staff. By modelling healthy work–life balance, leaders signal to their staff that it is okay to step back, recharge and prioritise personal health. When leaders demonstrate that they value self-care – by taking time off when needed, setting boundaries around work and openly discussing the importance of mental health – it gives permission for staff to do the same.

Self-care is not only vital for the wellbeing of school leaders but is also a crucial message to staff that taking care of oneself is not a luxury – it's a necessity. Leaders need to be the first to demonstrate this. Too often, there's an expectation that those in leadership roles should constantly be available, always working and never showing vulnerability. This mindset not only sets an unrealistic standard but also contributes to a toxic culture where overwork and burnout are normalised. Instead, leaders must model the behaviours they want to see in their staff by actively practising self-care. This could mean setting clear boundaries around working hours, encouraging staff to disconnect outside of work and being transparent about taking time off when needed. By doing so, leaders send a powerful message: wellbeing is not something to be sacrificed for productivity; it is, in fact, a key driver of long-term success.

For teachers, self-care can be particularly challenging. The profession is emotionally and physically demanding, and there is often an unspoken expectation that teachers will give every part of themselves to their work. This martyrdom mentality, where teachers are expected to stay late, take work home and prioritise students over their own needs, is unsustainable. Self-care needs to be actively promoted within schools, with leadership encouraging teachers to take breaks, use their vacation days and create clear work–life boundaries. Schools could even offer workshops or training on time management, stress reduction techniques or mindfulness to help staff develop strategies for balancing their personal and professional lives. These practices aren't just about reducing stress; they're about fostering a culture where staff feel empowered to take control of their own wellbeing, knowing they have the full support of the school behind them.

There is also the important matter of emotional labour – the energy required to manage one's own feelings while navigating the emotions of others. Teachers are constantly balancing the emotional needs of their students, colleagues and, often, parents, which can be draining. Leadership carries a similar burden, as leaders are tasked with managing the emotional climate of the entire school. Emotional labour can lead to significant stress and burnout if not managed carefully. Schools need to acknowledge the impact of emotional labour and offer resources to help staff manage it. This could include providing access to coaching, offering peer support groups where staff can share their experiences or even simply recognising the emotional toll that teaching can take and allowing space for staff to decompress after particularly difficult days or events.

In addition to self-care, creating a culture of shared responsibility for wellbeing is essential. Wellbeing cannot be something that is left solely to individual staff members to manage. It needs to be woven into the fabric of the school's culture. This means that wellbeing initiatives must be built into the school's day-to-day operations, not treated as add-ons. For instance, professional development sessions should include components on wellbeing, and regular staff meetings should feature check-ins on how people are feeling. Leaders should create opportunities for staff to come together and discuss what is working and what could be improved in terms of their wellbeing. By making wellbeing a regular part of school life, leaders can ensure that it remains a priority, rather than something that is only addressed when a crisis occurs.

One powerful tool for fostering this shared responsibility is peer support networks. These networks provide teachers with a space to connect with colleagues who are facing similar challenges, offering mutual support and advice. Peer networks can be formal or informal, but they should be actively encouraged by school leadership. Whether it's through regular meetups, online discussion groups or mentorship programmes, peer networks help to reduce feelings of isolation and build a sense of community within the school. They also provide a space for teachers to share best practices, troubleshoot common problems and simply vent about the frustrations of the job in a safe and supportive environment.

Empathy and Support are closely tied to building a strong sense of community within a school. When teachers feel that they are part of a supportive, collaborative team, they are far more likely to be resilient in the face of challenges. Schools should foster a sense of belonging by creating opportunities for staff to connect outside the classroom. This could be through social events, team-building activities or informal gatherings where staff can relax and build relationships. A sense of belonging not only improves staff morale but also strengthens the overall culture of the school, making it a more positive and supportive place to work. These connections are especially important during times of crisis, whether it's a global pandemic, a personal tragedy or a difficult school year. Having a strong support network in place helps staff navigate these challenges with greater ease.

As we look at fostering a culture of empathy, it's crucial to highlight that empathy is not just about feeling – it's about acting. Empathy in action means taking concrete steps to support staff when they need it most. This could involve adjusting workloads during particularly stressful periods, providing additional resources or time for teachers who are dealing with personal challenges, or simply offering a listening ear when someone needs to talk. Leadership should be proactive in identifying when staff may need extra support, rather than waiting for someone to reach breaking point before intervening. By being attuned to the emotional climate of the school, leaders can take preventive measures to address issues before they become crises, creating a more sustainable and supportive work environment.

Compassionate leadership has emerged as one of the most effective approaches for improving staff wellbeing. While empathy involves understanding and sharing the feelings of others, compassion takes it a step further by adding a desire to alleviate the suffering of others. Compassionate leadership involves actively seeking out ways to support staff, whether through practical solutions or emotional support. Leaders who demonstrate compassion not only build trust with their staff but also create a culture where everyone feels valued and cared for. One notable example of compassionate leadership comes from Microsoft CEO Satya Nadella, who transformed the company's culture by focusing on empathy and compassion. Nadella's leadership style was marked by his understanding that innovation and success stem from creating an environment where people feel supported, valued and empowered. This lesson translates directly to schools, where compassionate leadership can lead to improved morale, greater staff retention and, ultimately, better student outcomes.

In the realm of education, compassionate leadership can take many forms. It might mean offering additional support to a teacher who is struggling with a challenging class, providing flexibility for staff members dealing with personal issues, or simply creating a school culture where it's okay to admit when things aren't going well. Compassionate leaders recognise that staff are human beings with their own needs, struggles and limitations, and they actively seek out ways to make their lives easier, not harder. This type of leadership fosters a culture of trust and respect, where staff feel safe to express their concerns, ask for help and be vulnerable without fear of judgement or repercussions.

At the same time, compassion must be balanced with accountability. Compassionate leadership does not mean lowering expectations or excusing poor performance. Instead, it means recognising when staff need help and providing the support they need to meet the high standards expected of them. By offering a combination of empathy, support and accountability, leaders can create an environment where staff feel both supported and motivated to do their best work. This balance is critical for maintaining both staff wellbeing and the overall effectiveness of the school.

The final piece of the puzzle is ensuring that all of these efforts – Communication, Appreciation, Growth and Development, Empathy and Support – are part of a cohesive, strategic approach to wellbeing. Too often, schools implement piecemeal initiatives that address specific issues but fail to create a sustainable, long-term wellbeing strategy. This leads to frustration when efforts don't seem to have the desired impact. Instead, schools must take a holistic approach to staff wellbeing, where each element of the CAGE framework is interconnected and mutually reinforcing. For example, open communication should lead to more tailored professional development opportunities, which in turn should foster a greater sense of appreciation and support among staff. When these elements are working together, schools create a culture where staff wellbeing is embedded in every aspect of the school's operations.

In this holistic approach, leadership plays a critical role. Leaders must be the champions of wellbeing, not only by setting the vision but by living it every day. This means modelling the behaviours they want to see in their staff – whether it's practising self-care, offering empathy and support or actively engaging in professional development. Leadership is about more than just making decisions; it's about setting the tone for the entire school culture. When leaders prioritise wellbeing, the rest of the staff will follow suit. But if leaders are seen to be stressed, overworked or disengaged, it sends a message to staff that their own wellbeing isn't important either.

Ultimately, the change we are calling for is not radical. It's about returning to the basics of human connection, understanding and support. The foundation of any school is its people, and if we want our schools to thrive, we must take care of those people. This is not about implementing trendy wellbeing initiatives or checking boxes on a policy document; it's about fundamentally rethinking how we treat our teachers and staff. It's about creating environments where people feel valued, supported and empowered to do their best work – both for themselves and for their students.

Index

A
Accessible leadership: 13, 92-93
Alan Mulally: 82
Amazon: 82-84
Ancelotti, Carlo: VIII, 3, 6-8, 24, 46-47, 65
Ardern, Jacinda: 156, 161, 173

B
Barclays: 165-167
Basecamp: 28-30
Blakely, Sara: 50-52, 58
Burnout: 8, 25, 33, 44, 80, 84, 89, 96, 99-100, 142, 146-147, 156, 170-171, 175-176, 183, 186

C
CAGE framework: 11-12, 21, 178, 189
Calendar: 13, 69, 89-90, 92, 96, 112, 175, 179
Collaborative culture: 145-147, 150
COVID-19: 10, 20-21, 62, 156

D
Differentiated support: 144-145, 152
Disconnect: 30, 95-96, 186
Dweck, Carol: 56-57

E
Early career teachers: 15, 144, 181

F
Feedback mechanisms: 13, 52, 87-88, 101, 113, 123, 179
Ferguson, Alex: Pages 47-48
Flexible PPA: 32, 35-40
Flexible work arrangements: 16, 166-169, 182-184
Flywheel effect: 1-2

G
General Electric: 137
Google: 1-2, 18, 24-25, 41, 97, 118-121

H
Health and fitness: 76
HubSpot: 125-128
Hybrid learning model: 139-140

I
Ibrahimović, Zlatan: VIII, 6-8, 65
Intent statement: 26-31, 54
IT systems: 13, 93-94

J
Jeff Bezos: 82-84
Jürgen Klopp: 91-92

K
Kerr, James: 48-50
Knight, Phil: 66

M
Manchester City: 136
Megan Rapinoe: 103
Mentorship programmes: 76, 128-130, 142-143
Microsoft: 85, 88, 94, 121-124, 138, 156-157, 188

N
NBA: 138
Nadella, Satya: 85-86, 156-157, 161, 188
New Zealand: 49, 104, 156
NextJump: 25
Nooyi, Indra: 44-46, 58, 86

Index

O
Ohana culture: 171-172

P
Parents' evenings: 13, 89, 97-98, 167
Peer recognition programs: 14, 110, 112, 126, 180
Personalised thank-you notes: 108-109
Phil Jackson: 3-4, 7-8
Protocols: 35-37

Q
Quality assurance: XI, 26, 37-42, 69-70, 78

R
Report writing: 98-99
Ritz-Carlton: 28, 105-106
Rodman, Dennis: 3-8

S
Salesforce: 171-172
Self-care: 185-186
Seligman, Martin: 65, 71

Serena Williams: 4-7
Simon Sinek: 52-54, 58
Spotify: 36
Staff meetings: 1, 56, 69, 73, 75, 80, 81-88, 96, 99-100, 107, 109-110, 114, 164, 187
Staff shout-out boards: 106-108

T
Teach First: 28-29
Teacher development plan: 15, 141, 181
Toronto Raptors: 138
Transparent decision-making: 91-92

U
Unilever: 157-158

W
Wellbeing ambassadors: XI, 162-166

Z
Zappos: 103

For Product Safety Concerns and Information please contact our EU representative GPSR@taylorandfrancis.com
Taylor & Francis Verlag GmbH, Kaufingerstraße 24, 80331 München, Germany

www.ingramcontent.com/pod-product-compliance
Lightning Source LLC
Chambersburg PA
CBHW071820230426
43670CB00013B/2510